BEGINN FRENCH DICTIONARY

Helen Davies and Françoise Holmes
Illustrated by John Shackell
Designed by Brian Robertson
Edited by Nicole Irving

Handlettering by Jack Potter
Additional designs by Kim Blundell
Editorial help from Anita Ganeri

Contents

Using this book

This book contains over 2,000 useful French words, with pictures to help you remember them. To help you identify words, nouns (naming words) are printed in roman lettering (*le livre*, book) and verbs (doing words), adjectives (describing words) and phrases in italics (*grand*, big).

Nouns

French nouns are either masculine or feminine (this is called their gender). The French word for "the" shows which gender a noun is. "The" is **le** when the word is masculine and **la** when it is feminine. When a noun begins with a vowel, **le** or **la** is shortened to **l'**. The gender of the noun is then shown in the word box beside the picture using these abbreviations: **(f)** feminine, **(m)** masculine. Look out too for these abbreviations: **(s)** singular and **(pl)** plural. In the plural, the word for "the" is **les** whatever the gender of the noun.

In French, nouns which describe what people do or what they are (e.g. dancer) often have a masculine and a feminine form. When they appear in the illustrated section of the book only the form which matches the picture is given, but both masculine and feminine forms are given in the alphabetical word list at the back.

Adjectives

Adjectives in French change their ending depending on whether the noun they are describing is masculine or feminine. Usually you add an **e** to the masculine form to make the feminine, but some common adjectives form the feminine in different ways. You can find out about these on page 97.

In the pictures the adjective matches the noun illustrated. However it is useful to learn both masculine and feminine forms, so both are given in the word box. When you see only one form, it means the masculine and feminine are the same.

Verbs

Throughout the book verbs appear in the infinitive ("to hide, to look for" in English). Most French verbs have infinitives ending in **er, ir** or **re.** You can find out how to use verbs on page 99 and there is a list of irregular verbs on page 102.

le danseur de ballet

maigre

chercher

3

Meeting people

Bonjour	Hello	**l'homme(m)**	man
Au revoir	Goodbye	**la femme**	woman
A tout à l'heure.*	See you later.	**le bébé**	baby
serrer la main à	to shake hands with	**le garçon**	boy
faire la bise à	to kiss	**la fille**	girl

présenter	to introduce	**Comment allez-vous?**	How are you?
l'amie(f)	friend (f)	**Très bien, merci.**	Very well, thank you.
l'ami(m)	friend (m)		
rencontrer	to meet		

*You can find the literal meaning of phrases and expressions in the Phrase explainer section on pages 106-9.

bavarder	to chat		
Oui	Yes		
Non	No		
D'accord.	I agree.		
dire	to say		
éclater de rire	to burst out laughing		

bavarder

Oui

Non

D'accord.

dire

éclater de rire

le nom

le prénom

Sylvie BRUN

le nom de famille

le nom	name
le prénom	first name
le nom de famille	surname
Comment t'appelles-tu?	What's your name?
Je m'appelle...	My name is...
Il s'appelle...	His name is...

Je m'appelle ...

Il s'appelle ...

Comment t'appelles-tu?

l'âge

Quel âge as-tu ?

jeune

vieux

plus âgé que

plus jeune que

le même âge que

J'ai dix-neuf ans.

l'âge(m)	age	**vieux (vieille)***	old
Quel âge as-tu?	How old are you?	**plus âgé(e) que**	older than
J'ai dix-neuf ans.	I'm nineteen.	**plus jeune que**	younger than
jeune	young	**le même âge que**	the same age as

***Vieux** is an irregular adjective: the masculine changes to **vieil** in front of an ''h'' or a vowel, and the feminine is **vieille**.

Families

la famille
le grand-père
la tante
le père
l'oncle
la mère
la grand-mère
le frère
la soeur
la cousine
le cousin

la famille	family	la grand-mère	grandmother
le père	father	la tante	aunt
la mère	mother	l'oncle (m)	uncle
le frère	brother	la cousine	cousin (f)
la soeur	sister	le cousin	cousin (m)
le grand-père	grandfather		

être parent de
le petit-fils
la petite-fille
le fils
la fille
le neveu
élever
aimer bien
la nièce

être parent(e) de	to be related to	la petite-fille	granddaughter
le fils	son	aimer bien	to be fond of
la fille	daughter	le neveu	nephew
élever	to bring up	la nièce	niece
le petit-fils	grandson		

la femme	wife
le mari	husband
les parents(m)	parents
aimer	to love
les enfants (s: l'enfant(m))	children
les jumeaux (s: le jumeau)	twin brothers
le fils unique	only son

la femme

le mari

les parents

aimer

les enfants

les jumeaux

le fils unique

la vie

l'enfance

le mariage

la naissance

naître

se marier

les noces

la mort

travailler

la vieillesse

mourir

l'enterrement

la vie	life	les noces(f)	wedding
la naissance	birth	travailler	to work
naître	to be born	la vieillesse	old age
l'enfance(f)	childhood	la mort	death
le mariage	marriage	mourir	to die
se marier	to get married	l'enterrement(m)	funeral

Appearance and personality

joli(e)	pretty
beau (belle)	handsome
fort(e)	strong
faible	weak
maigre	thin
mince	slim
gros(se)	fat

jolie

beau

fort

maigre

gros

faible

mince

avoir les cheveux blonds

être chauve

...les cheveux bruns

...les cheveux roux

...les cheveux raides

...les cheveux frisés

...une frange

...des nattes

avoir les cheveux blonds	to have blond hair	les cheveux frisés	curly hair
		une frange	a fringe
les cheveux bruns	brown hair	des nattes	plaits
les cheveux roux	red hair	être chauve	to be bald
les cheveux raides	straight hair		

poli(e)	polite
impoli(e)	rude
gentil(le)	nice
idiot(e)	silly
timide	shy
sympathique	friendly
drôle	funny
heureux (heureuse)	cheerful
malheureux (malheureuse)	miserable

le teint	complexion	porter la barbe	to have a beard
brun(e)	dark	porter des lunettes	to wear glasses
blond(e)	fair, blond	froncer les sourcils	to frown
les taches(f) de rousseur	freckles	sourire	to smile
porter la moustache	to have a moustache	rire	to laugh
		pleurer	to cry

9

Your body

la tête	head
les cheveux(m)	hair
la figure	face
la peau	skin
l'oeil(m)*	eye
la joue	cheek
le nez	nose
l'oreille(f)	ear
la bouche	mouth
la dent	tooth
la langue	tongue
la lèvre	lip
le cou	neck
le menton	chin

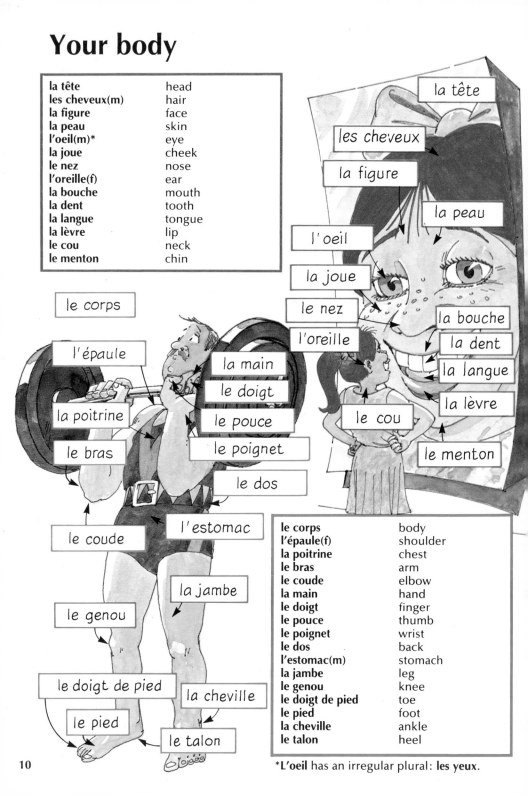

la tête

les cheveux

la figure

la peau

l'oeil

la joue

le nez

l'oreille

la bouche

la dent

la langue

la lèvre

le menton

le cou

le corps

l'épaule

la poitrine

le bras

la main

le doigt

le pouce

le poignet

le dos

le coude

l'estomac

la jambe

le genou

le doigt de pied

la cheville

le pied

le talon

le corps	body
l'épaule(f)	shoulder
la poitrine	chest
le bras	arm
le coude	elbow
la main	hand
le doigt	finger
le pouce	thumb
le poignet	wrist
le dos	back
l'estomac(m)	stomach
la jambe	leg
le genou	knee
le doigt de pied	toe
le pied	foot
la cheville	ankle
le talon	heel

***L'oeil** has an irregular plural: **les yeux**.

être grand(e)	to be tall
être petit(e)	to be short
se peser	to weigh yourself
peser peu	to be light
peser lourd	to be heavy

être grand

être petit

se peser

peser peu

peser lourd

le côté gauche

le côté droit

le côté gauche	left side
le côté droit	right side

s'agenouiller

s'allonger

être allongé

marcher pieds nus

être à genoux

s'asseoir

se lever

être debout

être assise

marcher pieds nus	to walk barefoot
se lever	to stand up
être debout	to be standing
s'agenouiller	to kneel down
être à genoux	to be kneeling
s'allonger	to lie down
être allongé(e)	to be lying down
s'asseoir	to sit down
être assis(e)	to be sitting down

Houses and homes

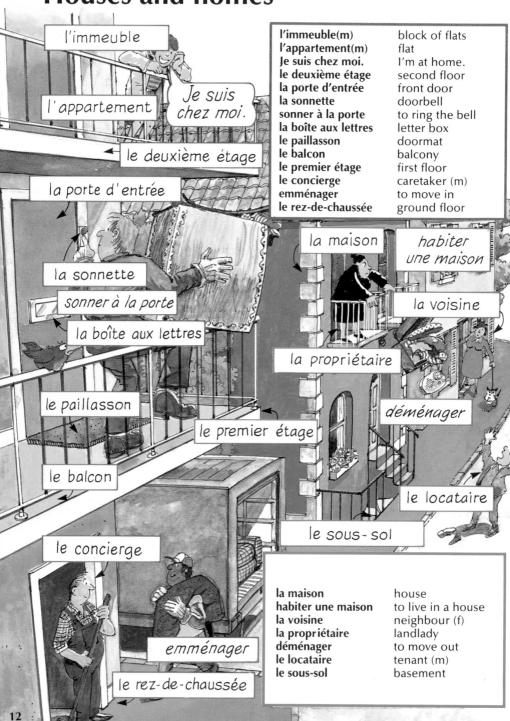

l'immeuble

l'appartement

Je suis chez moi.

le deuxième étage

la porte d'entrée

l'immeuble(m)	block of flats
l'appartement(m)	flat
Je suis chez moi.	I'm at home.
le deuxième étage	second floor
la porte d'entrée	front door
la sonnette	doorbell
sonner à la porte	to ring the bell
la boîte aux lettres	letter box
le paillasson	doormat
le balcon	balcony
le premier étage	first floor
le concierge	caretaker (m)
emménager	to move in
le rez-de-chaussée	ground floor

la sonnette

sonner à la porte

la boîte aux lettres

le paillasson

le balcon

le concierge

la maison

habiter une maison

la voisine

la propriétaire

déménager

le premier étage

le locataire

le sous-sol

emménager

le rez-de-chaussée

la maison	house
habiter une maison	to live in a house
la voisine	neighbour (f)
la propriétaire	landlady
déménager	to move out
le locataire	tenant (m)
le sous-sol	basement

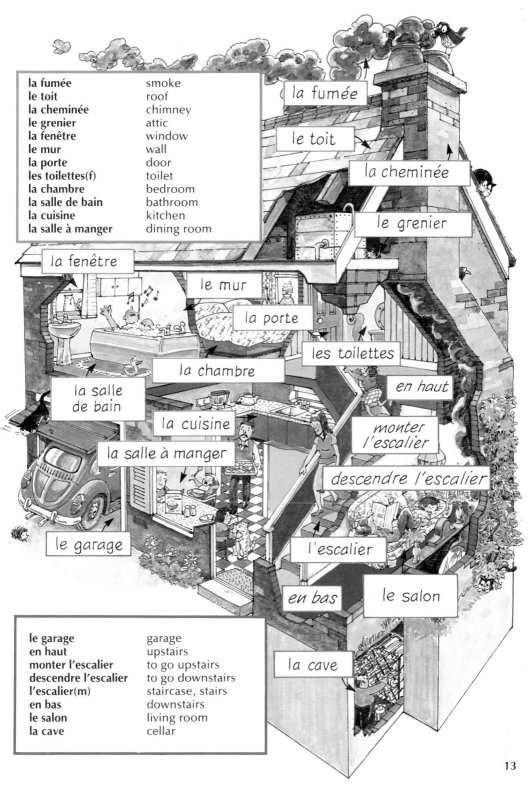

la fumée	smoke
le toit	roof
la cheminée	chimney
le grenier	attic
la fenêtre	window
le mur	wall
la porte	door
les toilettes(f)	toilet
la chambre	bedroom
la salle de bain	bathroom
la cuisine	kitchen
la salle à manger	dining room

la fumée

le toit

la cheminée

le grenier

la fenêtre

le mur

la porte

les toilettes

en haut

la chambre

la salle de bain

la cuisine

la salle à manger

monter l'escalier

descendre l'escalier

le garage

l'escalier

en bas

le salon

la cave

le garage	garage
en haut	upstairs
monter l'escalier	to go upstairs
descendre l'escalier	to go downstairs
l'escalier(m)	staircase, stairs
en bas	downstairs
le salon	living room
la cave	cellar

13

Dining room and living room

la salle à manger	dining room
la lumière	light
le radiateur	radiator
la table	table
la chaise	chair
le plancher	floor
le tapis	carpet

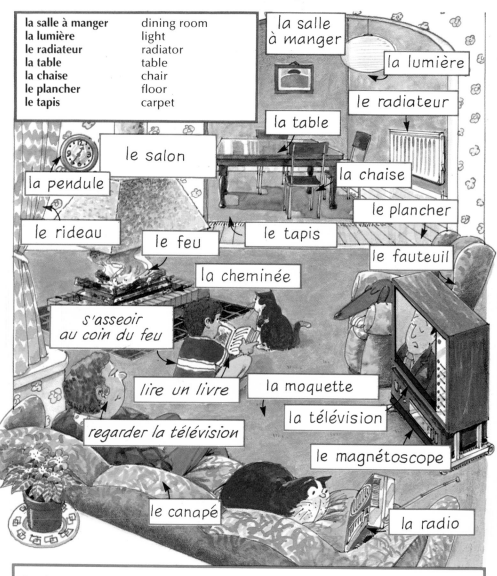

la salle à manger

la lumière

le radiateur

la table

la chaise

le plancher

le salon

la pendule

le rideau

le feu

le tapis

le fauteuil

la cheminée

s'asseoir au coin du feu

lire un livre

la moquette

la télévision

regarder la télévision

le magnétoscope

le canapé

la radio

le salon	living room	**lire un livre**	to read a book
la pendule	clock	**regarder la télévision**	to watch television
le rideau	curtain	**le canapé**	sofa
le feu	fire	**la moquette**	fitted carpet
la cheminée	fireplace	**la télévision**	television
le fauteuil	armchair	**le magnétoscope**	video
s'asseoir au coin du feu	to sit by the fire	**la radio**	radio

In the kitchen

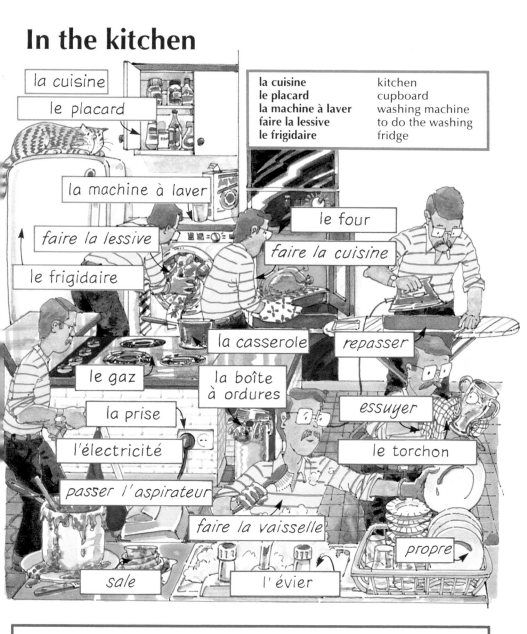

la cuisine

le placard

la cuisine	kitchen
le placard	cupboard
la machine à laver	washing machine
faire la lessive	to do the washing
le frigidaire	fridge

la machine à laver

le four

faire la lessive

faire la cuisine

le frigidaire

la casserole

repasser

le gaz

la boîte à ordures

essuyer

la prise

l'électricité

le torchon

passer l'aspirateur

faire la vaisselle

propre

sale

l'évier

le four	oven	**passer l'aspirateur**	to vacuum
faire la cuisine	to cook	**faire la vaisselle**	to wash up
la casserole	saucepan	**sale**	dirty
le gaz	gas	**l'évier(m)**	sink
la boîte à ordures	bin	**essuyer**	to dry, to wipe
repasser	to iron	**le torchon**	tea towel
la prise	plug	**propre**	clean
l'électricité(f)	electricity		

In the garden

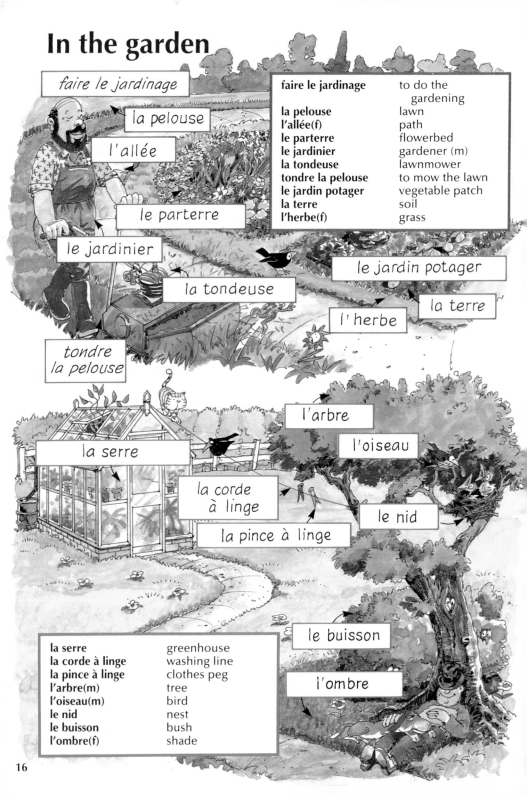

faire le jardinage

la pelouse

l'allée

le parterre

le jardinier

tondre
la pelouse

la tondeuse

l'herbe

le jardin potager

la terre

faire le jardinage	to do the gardening
la pelouse	lawn
l'allée(f)	path
le parterre	flowerbed
le jardinier	gardener (m)
la tondeuse	lawnmower
tondre la pelouse	to mow the lawn
le jardin potager	vegetable patch
la terre	soil
l'herbe(f)	grass

la serre

l'arbre

l'oiseau

la corde
à linge

la pince à linge

le nid

le buisson

l'ombre

la serre	greenhouse
la corde à linge	washing line
la pince à linge	clothes peg
l'arbre(m)	tree
l'oiseau(m)	bird
le nid	nest
le buisson	bush
l'ombre(f)	shade

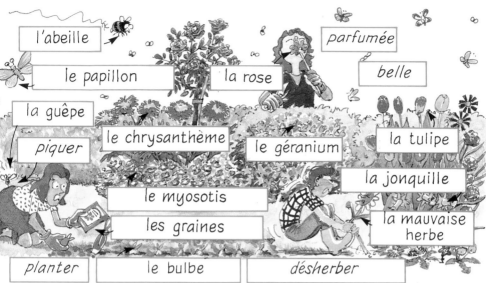

l'abeille(f)	bee	la tulipe	tulip
le papillon	butterfly	le myosotis	forget-me-not
la guêpe	wasp	la jonquille	daffodil
piquer	to sting	les graines(f)	seeds
la rose	rose	planter	to plant
parfumé(e)	sweet-smelling	le bulbe	bulb
beau (belle)	lovely, beautiful	désherber	to weed
le chrysanthème	chrysanthemum	la mauvaise herbe	weed
le géranium	geranium		

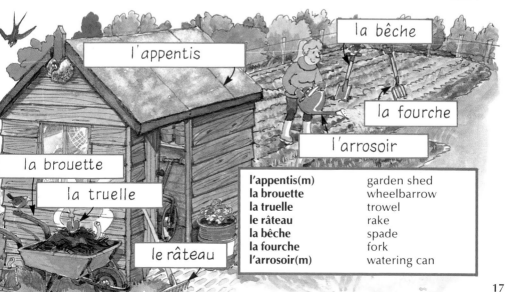

l'appentis(m)	garden shed
la brouette	wheelbarrow
la truelle	trowel
le râteau	rake
la bêche	spade
la fourche	fork
l'arrosoir(m)	watering can

Pets

le chien	dog
la niche	kennel
le petit chien	puppy
la fourrure	fur
la patte	paw
fou-fou	playful
aboyer	to bark
ATTENTION, CHIEN MECHANT	BEWARE OF THE DOG
courir après	to chase
aller chercher	to fetch
la queue	tail
remuer la queue	to wag its tail
gronder	to growl
promener le chien	to take the dog for a walk

le chien

la niche

le petit chien

la fourrure

la patte

fou-fou

aboyer

ATTENTION, CHIEN MECHANT

courir après

aller chercher

gronder

la queue

remuer la queue

promener le chien

le chat	cat
le panier	basket
ronronner	to purr
le chaton	kitten
miauler	to mew
s'étirer	to stretch
la griffe	claw
doux (douce)	soft
mignon(ne)	sweet

le chat

le panier

ronronner

le chaton

miauler

s'étirer

la griffe

doux

mignon

la perruche	budgie	**le lapin**	rabbit
se percher	to perch	**la tortue**	tortoise
l'aile(f)	wing	**la cage**	cage
le bec	beak	**donner à manger**	to feed
la plume	feather	**le poisson rouge**	goldfish
le hamster	hamster	**la souris**	mouse
le hérisson	hedgehog	**le bocal**	bowl
le cochon d'Inde	guinea pig		

la perruche

l'aile

se percher

le hamster

le bec

la plume

le hérisson

le cochon d'Inde

le lapin

la tortue

la cage

donner à manger

le poisson rouge

la souris

le bocal

19

Getting up

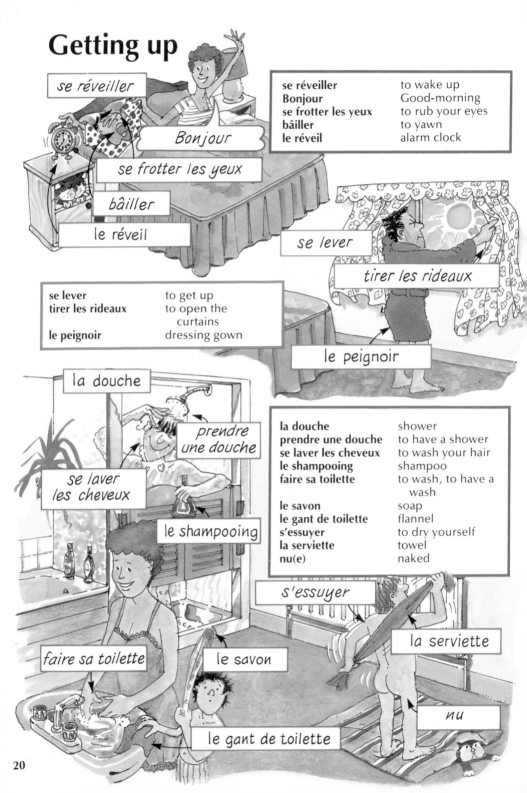

se réveiller

Bonjour

se frotter les yeux

bâiller

le réveil

se réveiller	to wake up
Bonjour	Good-morning
se frotter les yeux	to rub your eyes
bâiller	to yawn
le réveil	alarm clock

se lever

tirer les rideaux

se lever	to get up
tirer les rideaux	to open the curtains
le peignoir	dressing gown

le peignoir

la douche

prendre une douche

se laver les cheveux

le shampooing

la douche	shower
prendre une douche	to have a shower
se laver les cheveux	to wash your hair
le shampooing	shampoo
faire sa toilette	to wash, to have a wash
le savon	soap
le gant de toilette	flannel
s'essuyer	to dry yourself
la serviette	towel
nu(e)	naked

s'essuyer

la serviette

faire sa toilette

le savon

nu

le gant de toilette

20

se raser	to shave
la glace	mirror
le rasoir électrique	electric shaver
le rasoir	razor
la crème à raser	shaving foam

se raser

la glace

le rasoir électrique

le rasoir

la crème à raser

l'eau chaude

l'eau froide

le robinet

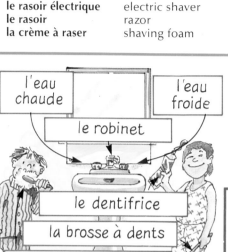

le dentifrice

la brosse à dents

se brosser les dents

le robinet	tap
l'eau(f) chaude	hot water
l'eau froide	cold water
le dentifrice	toothpaste
la brosse à dents	toothbrush
se brosser les dents	to clean your teeth

se sécher les cheveux	to dry your hair
le séchoir à cheveux	hairdrier
la brosse	brush
le peigne	comb
se peigner les cheveux	to comb your hair
se brosser les cheveux	to brush your hair

se sécher les cheveux

le séchoir à cheveux

la brosse

le peigne

se peigner les cheveux

se brosser les cheveux

se maquiller

le mascara

le fond de teint

le rouge à lèvres

le parfum

se maquiller	to put on make-up
le mascara	mascara
le fond de teint	foundation cream
le rouge à lèvres	lipstick
le parfum	perfume

Clothes

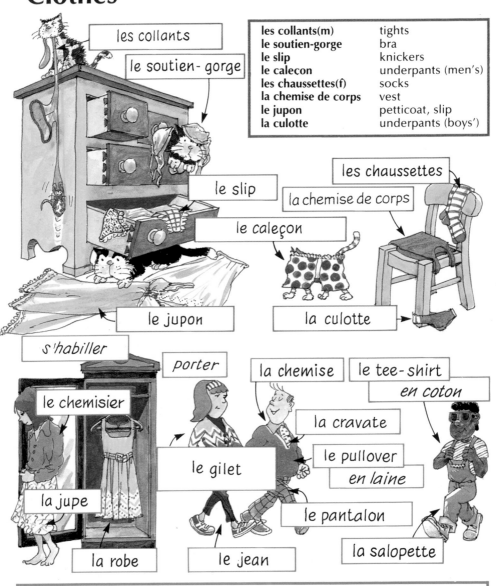

les collants

le soutien-gorge

les collants(m)	tights
le soutien-gorge	bra
le slip	knickers
le calecon	underpants (men's)
les chaussettes(f)	socks
la chemise de corps	vest
le jupon	petticoat, slip
la culotte	underpants (boys')

le slip

les chaussettes

la chemise de corps

le caleçon

le jupon

la culotte

s'habiller

porter

la chemise

le tee-shirt en coton

le chemisier

la cravate

le gilet

le pullover en laine

la jupe

le pantalon

la robe

le jean

la salopette

s'habiller	to get dressed	la cravate	tie
le chemisier	blouse	le pullover	jumper
la jupe	skirt	en laine	woollen
la robe	dress	le pantalon	trousers
porter	to wear	le tee-shirt	T-shirt
le gilet	cardigan	en coton	cotton, made of cotton
le jean	jeans		
la chemise	shirt	la salopette	dungarees

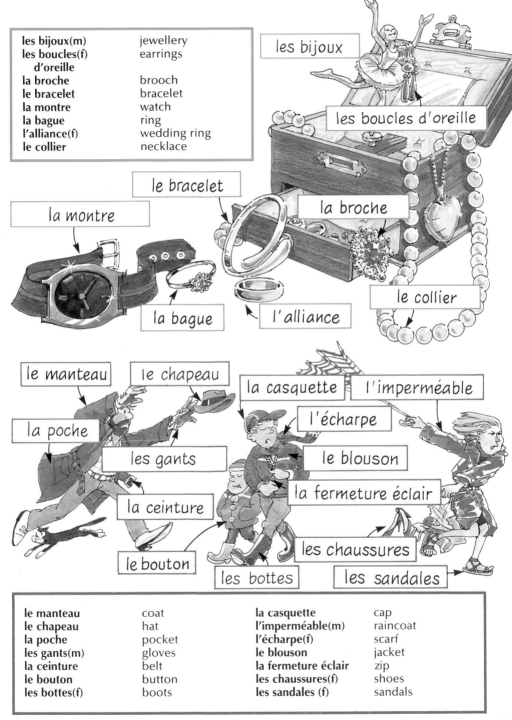

les bijoux(m)	jewellery
les boucles(f)	earrings
d'oreille	
la broche	brooch
le bracelet	bracelet
la montre	watch
la bague	ring
l'alliance(f)	wedding ring
le collier	necklace

les bijoux

les boucles d'oreille

le bracelet

la broche

la montre

le collier

la bague

l'alliance

le manteau

le chapeau

la casquette

l'imperméable

la poche

l'écharpe

les gants

le blouson

la ceinture

la fermeture éclair

le bouton

les chaussures

les bottes

les sandales

le manteau	coat	**la casquette**	cap
le chapeau	hat	**l'imperméable(m)**	raincoat
la poche	pocket	**l'écharpe(f)**	scarf
les gants(m)	gloves	**le blouson**	jacket
la ceinture	belt	**la fermeture éclair**	zip
le bouton	button	**les chaussures(f)**	shoes
les bottes(f)	boots	**les sandales (f)**	sandals

Going to bed

l'heure(f) d'aller se coucher	bedtime
allumer	to switch the light on
avoir sommeil	to be sleepy
ranger ses affaires	to tidy up
se déshabiller	to get undressed

l'heure d'aller se coucher

allumer

avoir sommeil

ranger ses affaires

se déshabiller

faire couler un bain

le bain

prendre un bain

le bouchon

le peignoir de bain

éclabousser

la descente de bain

la balance

faire couler un bain	to run a bath
prendre un bain	to have a bath
le bain	bath
le bouchon	plug
le peignoir de bain	bathrobe
éclabousser	to splash
la descente de bain	bathmat
la balance	scales

24

aller au lit

le pyjama

la chemise de nuit

les pantoufles

aller au lit	to go to bed
le pyjama	pyjamas
la chemise de nuit	nightdress
les pantoufles(f)	slippers

la berceuse

lire une histoire

le lit d'enfant

s'endormir

la berceuse	lullaby
lire une histoire	to read a story
le lit d'enfant	cot
s'endormir	to fall asleep

Bonne nuit.

Dormez bien.

rêver

ronfler

dormir

l'oreiller

éteindre

la lampe de chevet

le drap

la couette

le dessus-de-lit

la table de chevet

le lit

Bonne nuit.	Good-night.	la table de chevet	bedside table
Dormez bien.	Sleep well.	la couette	duvet
rêver	to dream	le lit	bed
dormir	to sleep	ronfler	to snore
éteindre	to switch the light off	l'oreiller(m)	pillow
		le drap	sheet
la lampe de chevet	bedside lamp	le dessus-de-lit	bedspread

25

Eating and drinking

mettre le couvert	to lay the table
A table!	It's ready!
la cafetière	coffee-pot
la théière	teapot
la serviette de table	napkin
le verre	glass
le bol	bowl
l'assiette(f)	plate
la tasse	cup
la soucoupe	saucer
la nappe	tablecloth
le pot	jug
la cuillère	spoon
le couteau	knife
la fourchette	fork

mettre le couvert

A table!

la cafetière

la théière

la serviette de table

le verre

la tasse

la cuillère

la soucoupe

le couteau

le bol

l'assiette

le pot

la fourchette

la nappe

Servez-vous.

Bon appétit!

avoir faim

avoir soif

manger

boire

C'est très bon.

avoir bien mangé

Servez-vous.	Help yourselves.
Bon appétit!	Enjoy your meal!
avoir soif	to be thirsty
boire	to drink
avoir faim	to be hungry
manger	to eat
C'est très bon.	It tastes good.
avoir bien mangé	to have eaten well

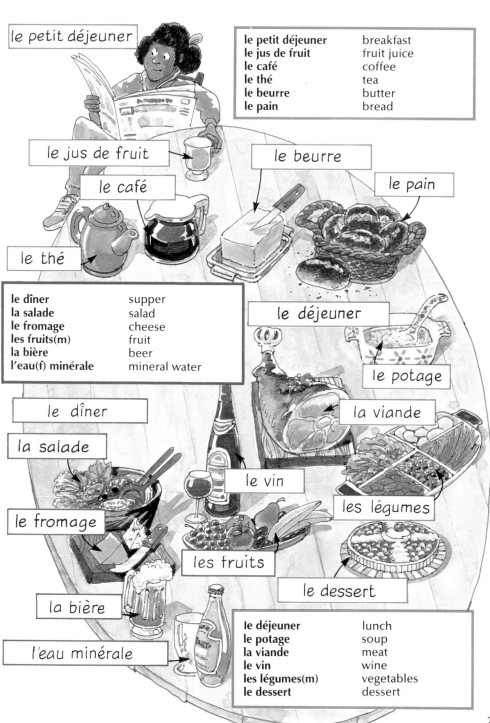

le petit déjeuner

le petit déjeuner	breakfast
le jus de fruit	fruit juice
le café	coffee
le thé	tea
le beurre	butter
le pain	bread

le jus de fruit

le beurre

le café

le pain

le thé

le dîner	supper
la salade	salad
le fromage	cheese
les fruits(m)	fruit
la bière	beer
l'eau(f) minérale	mineral water

le déjeuner

le potage

le dîner

la viande

la salade

le vin

le fromage

les légumes

les fruits

la bière

le dessert

l'eau minérale

le déjeuner	lunch
le potage	soup
la viande	meat
le vin	wine
les légumes(m)	vegetables
le dessert	dessert

27

Buying food

la viande

le pâté

le saucisson

le gigot d'agneau

la côte de porc

le bifteck

le poulet

le jambon

le veau

la saucisse

la viande	meat
le pâté	paté
le saucisson	French salami
le gigot d'agneau	leg of lamb
la côte de porc	pork chop
le poulet	chicken
le bifteck	steak
le jambon	ham
le veau	veal
la saucisse	sausage

le petit pois

les légumes

la carotte

la salade

frais

cru

les épinards

la tomate

le chou

l'ail

le chou-fleur

le haricot vert

la pomme de terre

l'oignon

le chou de Bruxelles

les légumes(m)	vegetables	**le chou-fleur**	cauliflower
frais (f: fraîche)	fresh	**le chou de Bruxelles**	Brussels sprout
le chou (pl: les choux)	cabbage	**la salade**	lettuce
l'ail(m)	garlic	**cru(e)**	raw
l'oignon(m)	onion	**la tomate**	tomato
le petit pois	pea	**le haricot vert**	green bean
la carotte	carrot	**la pomme de terre**	potato
les épinards(m)	spinach		

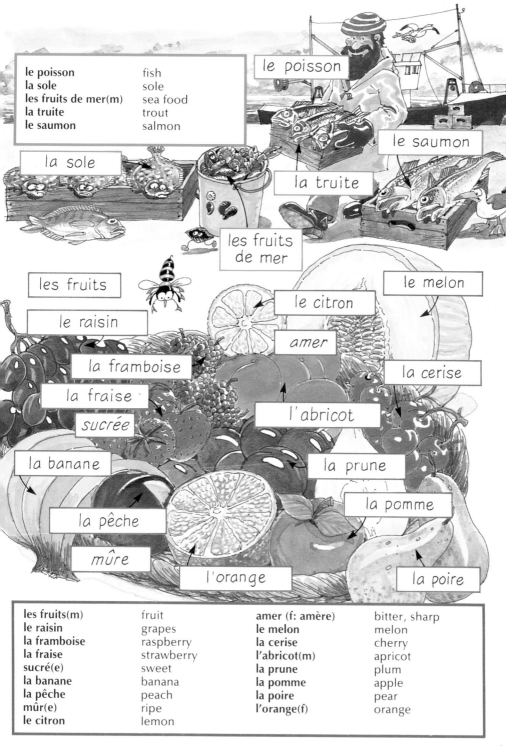

le poisson

le poisson	fish
la sole	sole
les fruits de mer(m)	sea food
la truite	trout
le saumon	salmon

le saumon

la sole

la truite

les fruits de mer

les fruits

le melon

le raisin

le citron

amer

la framboise

la cerise

la fraise

sucrée

l'abricot

la banane

la prune

la pêche

la pomme

mûre

l'orange

la poire

les fruits(m)	fruit	amer (f: amère)	bitter, sharp
le raisin	grapes	le melon	melon
la framboise	raspberry	la cerise	cherry
la fraise	strawberry	l'abricot(m)	apricot
sucré(e)	sweet	la prune	plum
la banane	banana	la pomme	apple
la pêche	peach	la poire	pear
mûr(e)	ripe	l'orange(f)	orange
le citron	lemon		

29

Buying food

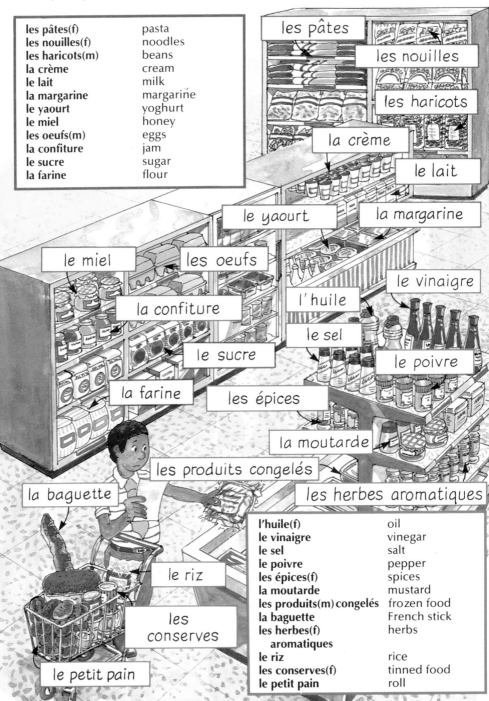

les pâtes(f) — pasta
les nouilles(f) — noodles
les haricots(m) — beans
la crème — cream
le lait — milk
la margarine — margarine
le yaourt — yoghurt
le miel — honey
les oeufs(m) — eggs
la confiture — jam
le sucre — sugar
la farine — flour

les pâtes
les nouilles
les haricots
la crème
le lait
le yaourt
la margarine
le miel
les oeufs
le vinaigre
la confiture
l'huile
le sel
le sucre
le poivre
la farine
les épices
la moutarde
les produits congelés
les herbes aromatiques
la baguette
le riz
les conserves
le petit pain

l'huile(f) — oil
le vinaigre — vinegar
le sel — salt
le poivre — pepper
les épices(f) — spices
la moutarde — mustard
les produits(m) congelés — frozen food
la baguette — French stick
les herbes(f) aromatiques — herbs
le riz — rice
les conserves(f) — tinned food
le petit pain — roll

le chocolat	chocolate
le biscuit	biscuit
la tarte	tart
le beignet	doughnut
le gâteau	cake
la glace	ice-cream
la pâtisserie	pastry

le chocolat

le biscuit

la tarte

le beignet

la pâtisserie

le gâteau

la glace

faire la cuisine

la recette

goûter

le goût

les ingrédients

mélanger

Délicieux!

faire la cuisine	to cook
la recette	recipe
les ingrédients(m)	ingredients
mélanger	to mix
goûter	to taste
le goût	flavour, taste
Délicieux!	Delicious!

31

Pastimes

regarder la télévision	to watch television
la chaîne	channel
l'émission(f)	programme
écouter la radio	to listen to the radio
les écouteurs(m)	headphones
taper du pied	to tap your feet

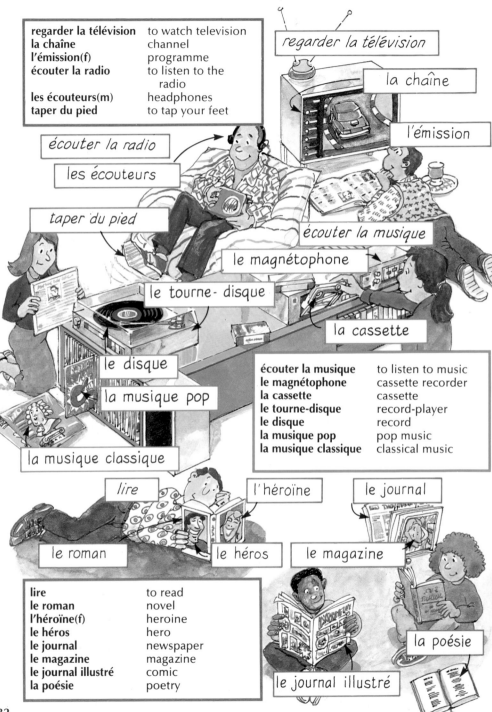

regarder la télévision

la chaîne

l'émission

écouter la radio

les écouteurs

taper du pied

écouter la musique

le magnétophone

le tourne-disque

la cassette

le disque

la musique pop

la musique classique

écouter la musique	to listen to music
le magnétophone	cassette recorder
la cassette	cassette
le tourne-disque	record-player
le disque	record
la musique pop	pop music
la musique classique	classical music

lire

l'héroïne

le journal

le roman

le héros

le magazine

la poésie

le journal illustré

lire	to read
le roman	novel
l'héroïne(f)	heroine
le héros	hero
le journal	newspaper
le magazine	magazine
le journal illustré	comic
la poésie	poetry

tricoter

les aiguilles
à tricoter

le patron

tricoter	to knit
les aiguilles(f) à tricoter	knitting needles
le patron	pattern
la laine	wool

la laine

coudre	to sew
le tissu	fabric
les ciseaux(m)	scissors
le fil	thread
l'épingle(f)	pin
l'aiguille(f)	needle
faire	to make

coudre

le tissu

le fil

faire

l'aiguille

les ciseaux

l'épingle

la menuiserie

le marteau

bricoler

adroite

réparer

le tournevis

la scie

fabriquer

la menuiserie	woodwork
bricoler	to do odd jobs
la scie	saw
fabriquer	to make, to manufacture
le marteau	hammer
adroit(e)	skilful, good with your hands
réparer	to mend
le tournevis	screwdriver

33

Pastimes

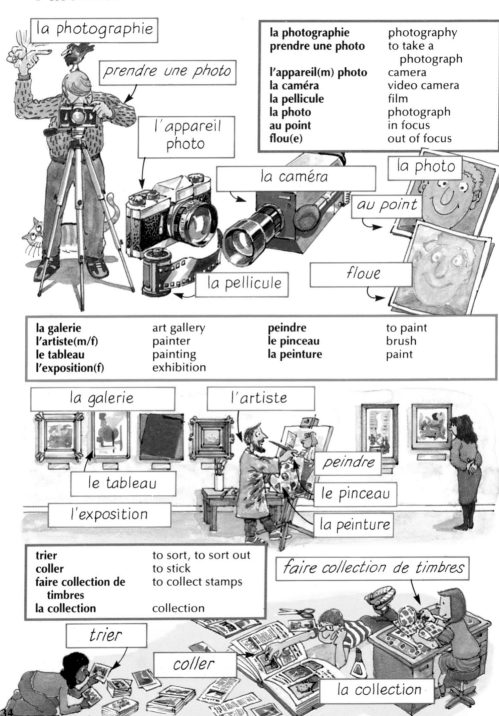

la photographie

prendre une photo

l'appareil photo

la photographie	photography
prendre une photo	to take a photograph
l'appareil(m) photo	camera
la caméra	video camera
la pellicule	film
la photo	photograph
au point	in focus
flou(e)	out of focus

la caméra

la photo

au point

floue

la pellicule

la galerie	art gallery	**peindre**	to paint
l'artiste(m/f)	painter	**le pinceau**	brush
le tableau	painting	**la peinture**	paint
l'exposition(f)	exhibition		

la galerie

l'artiste

le tableau

peindre

le pinceau

l'exposition

la peinture

trier	to sort, to sort out
coller	to stick
faire collection de timbres	to collect stamps
la collection	collection

faire collection de timbres

trier

coller

la collection

34

la musicienne	musician (f)	jouer du tambour	to play the drums
l'instrument(m)	instrument	jouer de la trompette	to play the trumpet
jouer du violon	to play the violin	jouer du violoncelle	to play the cello
jouer du piano	to play the piano	l'orchestre(m)	orchestra
jouer de la guitare	to play the guitar	le chef d'orchestre	conductor (m/f)

la musicienne

l'instrument

jouer du violon

jouer du piano

jouer de la guitare

jouer du tambour

jouer de la trompette

jouer du violoncelle

l'orchestre

le chef d'orchestre

chanter

l'air

chanter	to sing
l'air(m)	tune
le choeur	choir
chanter faux	to sing out of tune

chanter faux

le choeur

les jeux

jouer aux cartes

jouer aux dames

les jeux(m)	games
jouer aux cartes	to play cards
jouer aux dames	to play draughts
jouer aux échecs	to play chess
le jeu de société	board game

le jeu de société

jouer aux échecs

Going out

le cinéma	cinema
aller au cinéma	to go to the cinema
le film	film
la place	seat
l'ouvreuse(f)	usherette
le guichet	box-office

le cinéma

aller au cinéma

le film

l'ouvreuse

la place

le guichet

aller dans une boîte

le disc jockey

aller dans une boîte	to go to a discothèque
le disc jockey	disc jockey
danser	to dance
la piste de danse	dance floor

danser

la piste de danse

le théâtre

la pièce de théâtre

le décor

Bis !

l'actrice

le projecteur

l'acteur

la scène

les spectateurs

applaudir

beaucoup aimer

le théâtre	theatre
la pièce de théâtre	play
le décor	scenery
le projecteur	spotlight
l'actrice(f)	actress
l'acteur(m)	actor
la scène	stage
les spectateurs(m)	audience
applaudir	to clap
beaucoup aimer	to like, to enjoy
Bis!	Encore!

le ballet	ballet	**l'opéra(f)**	opera
le danseur de ballet	ballet dancer (m)	**le chanteur**	singer (m)
célèbre	famous	**le costume**	costume

le restaurant	restaurant	**le dessert**	dessert, pudding
le garçon	waiter	**l'addition(f)**	bill
la carte	menu	**Service compris?**	Is service included?
Que désirez-vous?	What would you like?		
		Service non compris!	Service not included!
commander	to order		
servir	to serve	**le pourboire**	tip
l'entrée(f)	starter	**le plateau**	tray
le plat principal	main course		

37

At the zoo

le zoo	zoo
l'animal(m)	animal
le zèbre	zebra
la girafe	giraffe
l'ours(m) blanc	polar bear
l'éléphant(m)	elephant
la trompe	trunk
la défense	tusk
le gorille	gorilla
sauvage	wild
apprivoisé(e)	tame
donner à manger	to feed
le gardien de zoo	zoo keeper (m)

le zoo

l'animal

le zèbre

la girafe

l'ours blanc

l'éléphant

la trompe

le gorille

sauvage

apprivoisé

la défense

donner à manger

le gardien de zoo

In the park

le parc	park
le bassin	pond
le canot à rames	rowing boat
ramer	to row
la rame	oar
le pique-nique	picnic
le banc	bench
se reposer	to rest

le parc

le bassin

la rame

le canot à rames

ramer

se reposer

le pique- nique

le banc

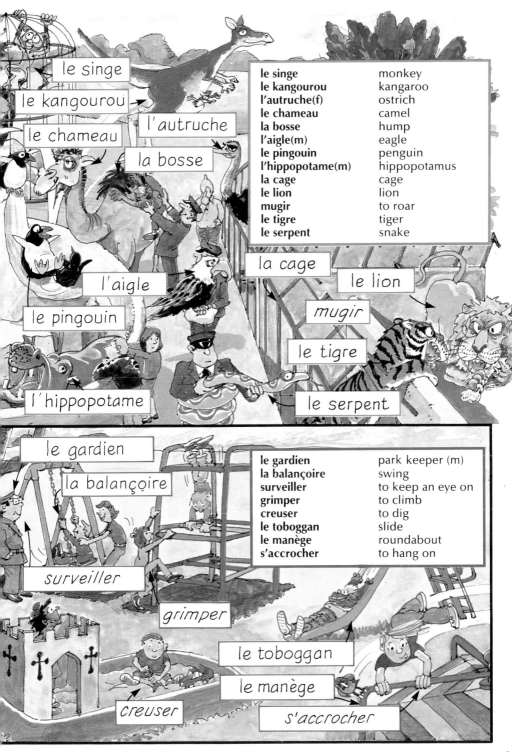

le singe

le kangourou

l'autruche

le chameau

la bosse

le singe	monkey
le kangourou	kangaroo
l'autruche(f)	ostrich
le chameau	camel
la bosse	hump
l'aigle(m)	eagle
le pingouin	penguin
l'hippopotame(m)	hippopotamus
la cage	cage
le lion	lion
mugir	to roar
le tigre	tiger
le serpent	snake

la cage

le lion

mugir

le tigre

l'aigle

le pingouin

l'hippopotame

le serpent

le gardien

la balançoire

le gardien	park keeper (m)
la balançoire	swing
surveiller	to keep an eye on
grimper	to climb
creuser	to dig
le toboggan	slide
le manège	roundabout
s'accrocher	to hang on

surveiller

grimper

le toboggan

le manège

creuser

s'accrocher

In the city

la grande ville

la banlieue

la ville

le pont

le gratte-ciel

le fleuve

la cathédrale

le quartier

le bâtiment

l'église

le cimetière

la grande ville	city
la banlieue	suburb
la ville	town
le gratte-ciel	skyscraper
la cathédrale	cathedral
le fleuve	river
le pont	bridge
le quartier	district
le bâtiment	building
l'église(f)	church
le cimetière	cemetery

la caserne de pompiers

l'hôtel de ville

le commissariat de police

les bureaux

la pompe à incendie

la voiture de police

l'usine

la bibliothèque

la caserne de pompiers	fire station	**les bureaux(m)**	offices, office block
la pompe à incendie	fire engine	**le commissariat de police**	police station
l'usine(f)	factory	**la voiture de police**	police car
l'hôtel(m) de ville	town hall	**la bibliothèque**	library

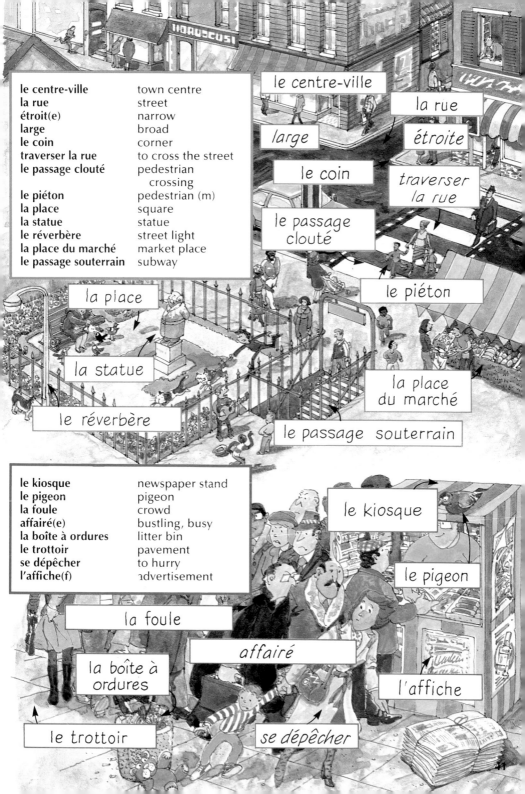

le centre-ville	town centre
la rue	street
étroit(e)	narrow
large	broad
le coin	corner
traverser la rue	to cross the street
le passage clouté	pedestrian crossing
le piéton	pedestrian (m)
la place	square
la statue	statue
le réverbère	street light
la place du marché	market place
le passage souterrain	subway

le centre-ville

la rue

large

étroite

le coin

traverser la rue

le passage clouté

le piéton

la place

la statue

la place du marché

le réverbère

le passage souterrain

le kiosque	newspaper stand
le pigeon	pigeon
la foule	crowd
affairé(e)	bustling, busy
la boîte à ordures	litter bin
le trottoir	pavement
se dépêcher	to hurry
l'affiche(f)	advertisement

le kiosque

le pigeon

la foule

affairé

la boîte à ordures

l'affiche

le trottoir

se dépêcher

Shopping

faire une liste

le sac à provisions

les magasins

faire les courses

la charcuterie

la boulangerie

la boucherie

l'épicerie

| faire une liste | to make a list |
| le sac à provisions | shopping bag |

la poissonnerie

la mercerie

la pâtisserie

la pharmacie

la librairie

le fleuriste

le marchand de disques

le coiffeur

la boutique

les magasins(m)	shops	**la pharmacie**	chemist
faire les courses	to go shopping	**la librairie**	bookshop
la boucherie	butcher	**la mercerie**	needlecraft shop
la charcuterie	delicatessen	**le fleuriste**	florist
l'épicerie(f)	grocery shop	**le coiffeur**	hairdresser
la boulangerie	bakery	**le marchand de**	record shop
la pâtisserie	cake shop	**disques**	
la poissonnerie	fishmonger	**la boutique**	boutique

faire le marché

l'étalage

faire la queue

Ça fait...

Combien je vous dois?

peser

Un kilo de...

Une livre de...

faire le marché	to shop at the market
l'étalage(m)	market stall
faire la queue	to queue

Combien je vous dois?	How much do I owe you?
Ça fait...	That will be...
peser	to weigh
Un kilo de...	A kilo of...
Une livre de...	Half a kilo of...

aller au supermarché

le haut-parleur

le panier

le comptoir

la boîte

l'allée

le paquet

le chariot

la bouteille

l'entrée

la sortie

la caisse

le sac

la caissière

aller au supermarché	to go to the supermarket
le panier	basket
le chariot	trolley
le haut-parleur	loudspeaker
le comptoir	counter
l'allée(f)	aisle
la boîte	tin
le paquet	packet
la bouteille	bottle
l'entrée(f)	entrance
la sortie	exit
la caisse	checkout
le sac	carrier-bag
la caissière	cashier (f)

Shopping

faire du lèche-vitrines	to go window-shopping	**SOLDE**	SALE
la vitrine	window display, shop window	**une bonne affaire**	a bargain
		la cliente	customer (f)
C'est bon marché.	It's good value.	**acheter**	to buy
C'est cher.	It's expensive.	**la vendeuse**	shop assistant (f)
		vendre	to sell

dépenser de l'argent	to spend money	**petit**	small
le prix	price	**moyen**	medium
le reçu	receipt	**grand**	large
Vous désirez?	Can I help you?	**Combien coûte...?**	How much is...?
Je voudrais...	I would like...	**Ça coûte...**	It costs...
C'est quelle taille?	What size is this?		

la librairie-papeterie	bookshop and stationer's	la carte postale	postcard
le livre	book	le stylo-bille	ball-point pen
le livre de poche	paperback	le crayon	pencil
l'enveloppe(f)	envelope	le papier à lettres	writing paper

la librairie-papeterie

l'enveloppe

la carte postale

le livre

le stylo-bille

le crayon

le livre de poche

le papier à lettres

le grand magasin

le rayon

l'ascenseur

l'escalier roulant

Jouets

Équipement de sport

Ameublement

Vêtements

le grand magasin	department store	Jouets(m.pl)	Toys
le rayon	department	Ameublement(m)	Furniture
l'escalier(m) roulant	escalator	Equipement de sport(m)	Sports equipment
l'ascenseur(m)	lift	Vêtements(m.pl)	Clothes

45

At the post office and bank

la poste	post office	**le télégramme**	telegram
la boîte aux lettres	post-box	**la fiche**	form
mettre à la poste	to post	**le timbre**	stamp
la lettre	letter	**par avion**	airmail
le colis	parcel	**l'adresse(f)**	address
heures de levée(f.pl)	collection times	**le code postal**	postal code
envoyer	to send		

la poste

envoyer

le télégramme

la boîte aux lettres

mettre à la poste

la fiche

la lettre

le colis

heures de levée

le timbre

par avion

l'adresse

le facteur

le code postal

le courrier

distribuer

le facteur	postman
le courrier	mail
distribuer	to deliver

la banque

le caissier

l'argent

Avez-vous de la petite monnaie ?

changer de l'argent

la pièce de monnaie

le cours du change

le directeur de banque

le billet

la carte de crédit

mettre de l'argent en banque

retirer de l'argent

le portefeuille

le carnet de chèques

faire un chèque

le portemonnaie

le sac à main

la banque	bank	le billet	note
l'argent(m)	money	la carte de crédit	credit card
changer de l'argent	to change money	mettre de l'argent en	to put money in
le cours du change	exchange rate	banque	the bank
le directeur de	bank manager	retirer de l'argent	to take money out
banque		le carnet de chèques	cheque-book
le caissier	cashier (m)	faire un chèque	to write a cheque
Avez-vous de la	Have you any	le portefeuille	wallet
petite monnaie?	small change?	le portemonnaie	purse
la pièce de monnaie	coin	le sac à main	handbag

47

Phonecalls and letters

téléphoner	to make a telephone call	**l'annuaire(m)**	telephone directory
le téléphone	telephone	**sonner**	to ring
le récepteur	receiver	**répondre au téléphone**	to answer the telephone
décrocher	to pick up the receiver	**Allô...**	Hello...
composer le numéro	to dial the number	**qui est à l'appareil?**	who's speaking?
le numéro de téléphone	telephone number	**C'est Jeanne.**	It's Jeanne.
l'indicatif(m)	area code	**Je te rappellerai.**	I'll call you back.
		Au revoir	Goodbye
		raccrocher	to hang up

la cabine téléphonique	telephone box
la catastrophe	emergency
appeler police secours	to dial 999

écrire une lettre

> Monsieur/Madame,   le 12 mars 1988
> Je vous remercie de votre lettre du…
> Veuillez trouver ci-joint…
> …par retour du courrier.
> Je vous prie de croire, Monsieur/Madame,
> à mes sentiments
> les meilleurs.

écrire une lettre	to write a letter	**par retour du courrier**	by return
Monsieur/Madame,	Dear Sir/Madam,	**Je vous prie de croire,**	Yours faithfully,
Je vous remercie de votre lettre du…	Thank you for your letter of…	**Monsieur/Madame, à mes sentiments**	
Veuillez trouver ci-joint...	Please find enclosed…	**les meilleurs.**	

ouvrir une lettre

> Chère Jeanne,   samedi 9 janvier 1999
> J'ai été très content
> d'avoir de tes nouvelles
> Je t'envoie… séparément.
> Bons baisers,

ouvrir une lettre	to open a letter	**Je t'envoie…**	I am sending…
Chère Jeanne,	Dear Jeanne,	**séparément.**	separately.
J'ai été très content(e) d'avoir de tes nouvelles.	It was lovely to hear from you.	**Bons baisers,**	Love from…

envoyer une carte postale

envoyer un télégramme

> Nous nous amusons beaucoup.
> Je pense bien à toi.

> Message urgent
> stop appelle
> maison

envoyer une carte postale	to send a postcard	**envoyer un télégramme**	to send a telegram
Nous nous amusons beaucoup.	Having a lovely time.	**Message urgent stop appelle maison**	Urgent message stop phone home
Je pense bien à toi.	Thinking of you.		

Out and about

aller à pied	to walk	**la carte**	map
courir	to run	**le poteau indicateur**	signpost
la poussette	push-chair	**Est-ce que... est loin d'ici?**	Is it far to...?
Pour aller à...?	Which way is...?		
demander le chemin	to ask the way		

prendre l'autobus	to take the bus	**l'autobus(m)**	bus
le passager	passenger (m)	**l'arrêt(m) d'autobus**	bus stop
descendre de	to get off	**la station de métro**	underground station
monter dans	to get on		
le billet	ticket	**le métro**	underground

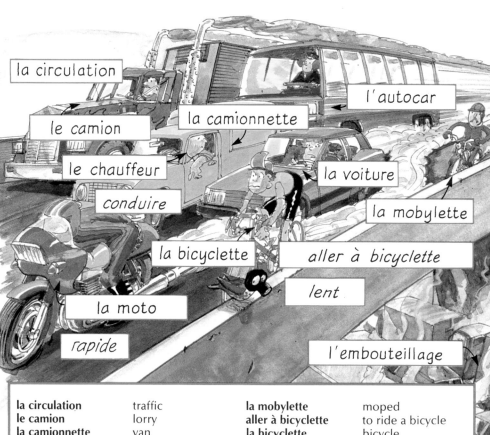

la circulation

le camion

la camionnette

l'autocar

le chauffeur

la voiture

conduire

la mobylette

la bicyclette

aller à bicyclette

lent

la moto

rapide

l'embouteillage

la circulation	traffic	la mobylette	moped
le camion	lorry	aller à bicyclette	to ride a bicycle
la camionnette	van	la bicyclette	bicycle
l'autocar(m)	coach	lent(e)	slow
le chauffeur	driver (m/f)	la moto	motorbike
conduire	to drive	rapide	fast
la voiture	car	l'embouteillage(m)	traffic jam

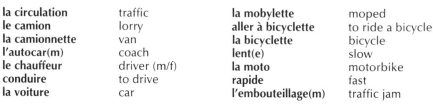

la station de taxis

le taxi

appeler un taxi

le prix de la course

la station de taxis	taxi rank
le taxi	taxi
appeler un taxi	to hail a taxi
le prix de la course	fare

Driving

démarrer

doubler

l'autoroute

les feux

la route

ralentir

accélérer

tourner à gauche

tourner à droite

aller tout droit

la rue

sens unique

sens interdit

démarrer	to start off
accélérer	to gather speed
doubler	to overtake
ralentir	to slow down
l'autoroute(f)	motorway
les feux(m)	traffic lights
la route	main road, road
tourner à gauche	to turn left
tourner à droite	to turn right
aller tout droit	to go straight on
la rue	side street, street
sens unique	one way
sens interdit	no entry

le parking

garer la voiture

en arrière

Stationnement interdit!

en avant

Stationnement interdit!	No parking!	garer la voiture	to park
		en arrière	backwards
le parking	car-park	en avant	forwards

la collision	collision
le volant	steering wheel
le pare-brise	windscreen
la ceinture de sécurité	safety belt
le clignotant	indicator
le phare	headlight
le capot	bonnet
le coffre	boot
la plaque d'immatriculation	number plate
la roue	wheel
le pneu	tyre
le klaxon	horn

la collision

le volant

le pare-brise

la ceinture de sécurité

le clignotant

le phare

le capot

le coffre

la plaque d'immatriculation

la roue

le pneu

avoir un pneu crevé

tomber en panne

le klaxon

l'huile

le mécanicien

la station-service

faire le plein

l'essence

avoir un pneu crevé	to have a flat tyre
tomber en panne	to have a breakdown
le mécanicien	mechanic (m)
l'huile(f)	oil
la station-service	petrol station
faire le plein	to fill up with petrol
l'essence(f)	petrol

53

Travelling by train

la gare

la consigne

le porteur

le contrôleur

la salle d'attente

la barrière

le voyageur

l'horaire

Le train à destination de ...

le guichet

Le train en provenance de ...

le billet

le billet aller retour

la carte d'abonnement

le distributeur automatique

réserver une place

le ticket de quai

la gare	station	Le train en provenance de...	The train from...
le porteur	porter		
la consigne	left luggage office	le guichet	ticket office
le contrôleur	ticket collector (m)	le billet	ticket
la salle d'attente	waiting-room	le billet aller retour	return ticket
la barrière	barrier	la carte d'abonnement	season ticket
le voyageur	traveller (m)	le distributeur automatique	ticket machine
l'horaire(f)	timetable		
Le train à destination de...	The train to...	le ticket de quai	platform ticket
		réserver une place	to reserve a seat

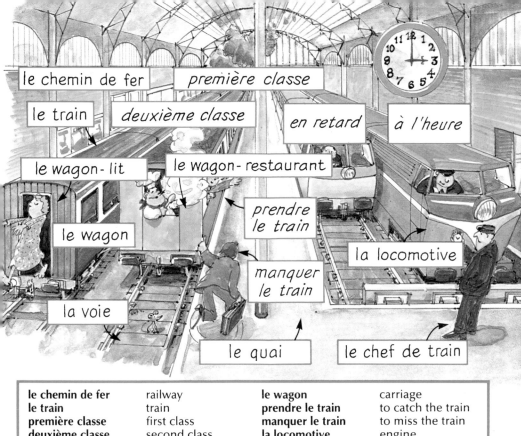

le chemin de fer

première classe

le train

deuxième classe

en retard

à l'heure

le wagon-lit

le wagon-restaurant

prendre le train

la locomotive

le wagon

manquer le train

la voie

le quai

le chef de train

le chemin de fer	railway	**le wagon**	carriage
le train	train	**prendre le train**	to catch the train
première classe	first class	**manquer le train**	to miss the train
deuxième classe	second class	**la locomotive**	engine
en retard	late	**la voie**	track
à l'heure	on time	**le quai**	platform
le wagon-lit	sleeping-car	**le chef de train**	guard
le wagon-restaurant	buffet car		

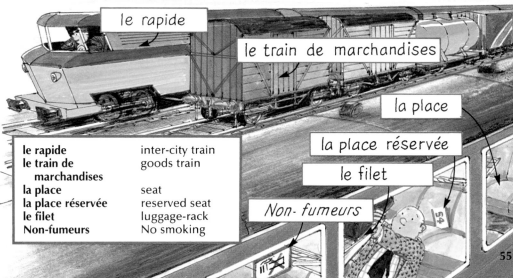

le rapide

le train de marchandises

la place

la place réservée

le filet

Non-fumeurs

le rapide	inter-city train
le train de marchandises	goods train
la place	seat
la place réservée	reserved seat
le filet	luggage-rack
Non-fumeurs	No smoking

Travelling by plane and boat

l'aéroport

l'avion

Arrivées

voler

la piste

atterrir

décoller

la douane

le douanier

Rien à déclarer

le passeport

l'aéroport(m)	airport
l'avion(m)	aeroplane
voler	to fly
Arrivées	Arrivals
la piste	runway
atterrir	to land
décoller	to take off

la douane	customs
le douanier	customs officer (m/f)
Rien à déclarer	Nothing to declare
le passeport	passport

le port

aller en bateau

le navire

le paquebot

la cheminée

le drapeau

la cabine

le capitaine

le hublot

le pont

l'ancre

la passerelle

le port	port	l'ancre(f)	anchor
aller en bateau	to travel by boat	la cabine	cabin
le navire	ship	le pont	deck
le paquebot	liner	la cheminée	funnel
le drapeau	flag	le capitaine	captain
le hublot	porthole	la passerelle	gangway

Départs	Departures	le pilote	pilot
le magasin hors-taxe	duty-free shop	l'équipage(m)	crew
l'enregistrement(m)	check-in	l'hôtesse(f) de l'air	air hostess
le billet d'avion	airline ticket	embarquer	to board
l'étiquette(f)	label	la valise	suitcase
le chariot	trolley	les bagages(m) à	hand luggage
Attachez vos	Fasten your	main	
ceintures.	seatbelts.		

Départs

le magasin hors-taxe

Attachez vos ceintures.

l'enregistrement

le pilote

l'équipage

l'hôtesse de l'air

la valise

le billet d'avion

embarquer

l'étiquette

le chariot

les bagages à main

le carferry

le dock

la traversée

avoir le mal de mer

la cargaison

charger

décharger

la cale

le marin

le carferry	ferry
la traversée	crossing
avoir le mal de mer	to be seasick
le dock	docks
la cargaison	cargo
charger	to load
décharger	to unload
la cale	hold
le marin	sailor

57

Holidays

aller en vacances

la touriste

faire sa valise

aller en vacances	to go on holiday
faire sa valise	to pack
la crème solaire	suntan lotion
les lunettes(f) de soleil	sunglasses
la touriste	tourist (f)
visiter	to visit, to sightsee

la crème solaire

les lunettes de soleil

visiter

rester à l'hôtel

l'hôtel

la réception

le porteur

avec salle de bain

une chambre à un lit

avec balcon

une chambre pour deux personnes

réserver une chambre

la pension

complet

l'hôtel(m)	hotel	**réserver une chambre**	to reserve a room
rester à l'hôtel	to stay in a hotel	**complet**	fully booked
la réception	reception	**avec salle de bain**	with bathroom
le porteur	porter	**avec balcon**	with balcony
une chambre à un lit	single room	**la pension**	guest house
une chambre pour deux personnes	double room		

au bord de la mer

la mouette

le maître nageur

la vague

le hors-bord

faire du ski nautique

faire de la planche à voile

se baigner

barboter

la mer

le sable

la plage

se bronzer

bronzé

le parasol

le château de sable

le seau

la pelle

le rocher

l'algue

le crabe

le coquillage

au bord de la mer	at the seaside
la mouette	seagull
le maître nageur	lifeguard
la vague	wave
le hors-bord	powerboat
faire du ski nautique	to waterski
faire de la planche à voile	to windsurf
se baigner	to swim, to have a swim
barboter	to paddle
la mer	sea
le sable	sand
la plage	beach

se bronzer	to sunbathe
bronzé(e)	tanned
le parasol	sunshade
le château de sable	sandcastle
le seau	bucket
la pelle	spade

le rocher	rock
l'algue(f)	seaweed
le crabe	crab
le coquillage	shell

59

Holidays

faire de l'alpinisme	to go mountaineering
la montagne	mountain
le sommet	summit
la vue	view
escarpé(e)	steep
escalader	to climb
l'alpiniste(m or f)	climber
le sac à dos	rucksack, backpack

faire du ski

la station de ski

le sommet

faire de l'alpinisme

le télésiège

la montagne

la vue

escalader

escarpé

l'alpiniste

le sac à dos

le moniteur

la piste

la luge

le bâton de ski

les chaussures de ski

les skis

faire du ski	to go skiing
la station de ski	ski resort
le télésiège	chairlift
le moniteur	ski instructor
la piste	ski slope, ski run
la luge	sledge
le bâton de ski	ski pole
les chaussures(f) de ski	ski boots
les skis(m)	skis

60

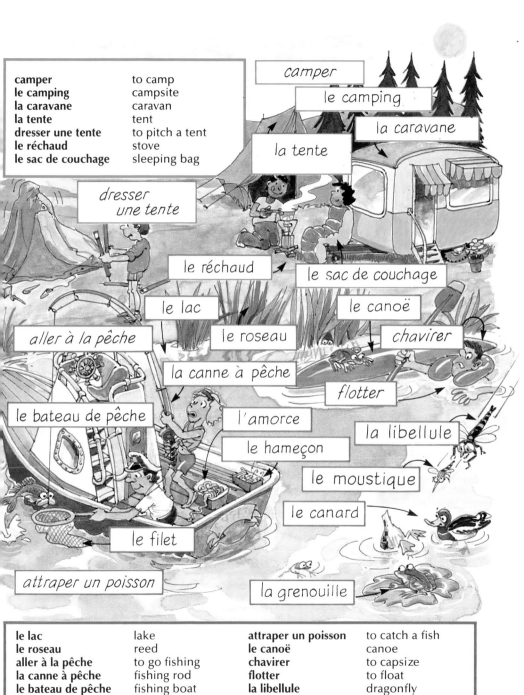

camper	to camp
le camping	campsite
la caravane	caravan
la tente	tent
dresser une tente	to pitch a tent
le réchaud	stove
le sac de couchage	sleeping bag

camper

le camping

la caravane

la tente

dresser une tente

le réchaud

le lac

le sac de couchage

le canoë

aller à la pêche

le roseau

chavirer

la canne à pêche

flotter

le bateau de pêche

l'amorce

la libellule

le hameçon

le moustique

le canard

le filet

attraper un poisson

la grenouille

le lac	lake	**attraper un poisson**	to catch a fish
le roseau	reed	**le canoë**	canoe
aller à la pêche	to go fishing	**chavirer**	to capsize
la canne à pêche	fishing rod	**flotter**	to float
le bateau de pêche	fishing boat	**la libellule**	dragonfly
l'amorce(f)	bait	**le moustique**	mosquito
le hameçon	hook	**le canard**	duck
le filet	net	**la grenouille**	frog

In the countryside

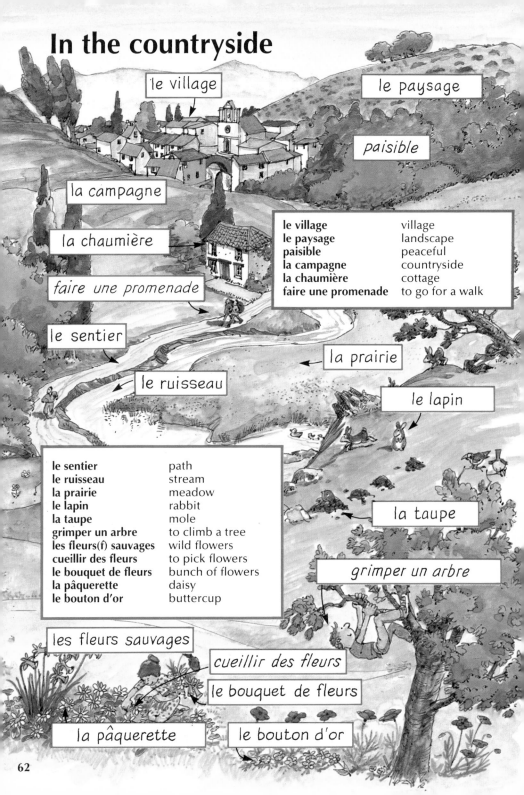

le village

le paysage

paisible

la campagne

la chaumière

faire une promenade

le sentier

la prairie

le ruisseau

le lapin

le village	village
le paysage	landscape
paisible	peaceful
la campagne	countryside
la chaumière	cottage
faire une promenade	to go for a walk

le sentier	path
le ruisseau	stream
la prairie	meadow
le lapin	rabbit
la taupe	mole
grimper un arbre	to climb a tree
les fleurs(f) sauvages	wild flowers
cueillir des fleurs	to pick flowers
le bouquet de fleurs	bunch of flowers
la pâquerette	daisy
le bouton d'or	buttercup

la taupe

grimper un arbre

les fleurs sauvages

cueillir des fleurs

le bouquet de fleurs

la pâquerette

le bouton d'or

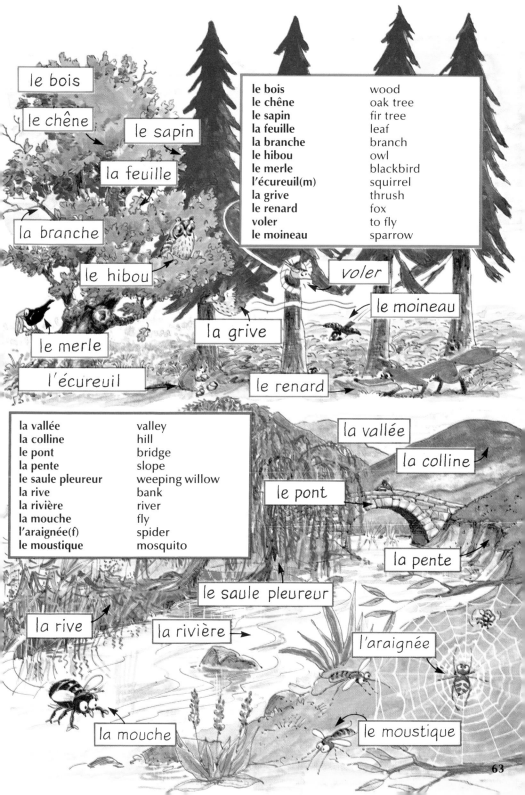

le bois

le chêne

le sapin

la feuille

la branche

le hibou

le bois	wood
le chêne	oak tree
le sapin	fir tree
la feuille	leaf
la branche	branch
le hibou	owl
le merle	blackbird
l'écureuil(m)	squirrel
la grive	thrush
le renard	fox
voler	to fly
le moineau	sparrow

voler

le moineau

la grive

le merle

l'écureuil

le renard

la vallée	valley
la colline	hill
le pont	bridge
la pente	slope
le saule pleureur	weeping willow
la rive	bank
la rivière	river
la mouche	fly
l'araignée(f)	spider
le moustique	mosquito

la vallée

la colline

le pont

la pente

le saule pleureur

la rive

la rivière

l'araignée

la mouche

le moustique

63

On the farm

la ferme

l' étable

l' écurie

le cheval

la grange

le foin

la vache

l'âne

traire les vaches

le cochon

le veau

l'échelle

le coq

la ferme

la basse - cour

la poule

le poulailler

pondre des oeufs

la fermière

l'oie

la chèvre

la ferme	farm	**l'échelle(f)**	ladder
l'étable(f)	cowshed	**la ferme**	farmhouse
l'écurie(f)	stable	**la basse-cour**	farmyard
le cheval	horse	**la poule**	hen
la grange	barn	**le coq**	cock
le foin	hay	**le poulailler**	henhouse
la vache	cow	**pondre des oeufs**	to lay eggs
traire les vaches	to milk the cows	**la fermière**	farmer (f), farmer's
le veau	calf		wife
l'âne(m)	donkey	**l'oie(f)**	goose
le cochon	pig	**la chèvre**	goat

le champ

le troupeau

le champ	field
le troupeau	flock
le mouton	sheep
l'agneau(m)	lamb
le fermier	farmer
la barrière	gate
le chien de berger	sheepdog

le mouton

l'agneau

la barrière

le chien de berger

le fermier

le vignoble	vineyard
la vigne	vine
faire la moisson	to harvest
la meule de foin	haystack
le blé	wheat
semer	to sow

le vignoble

la vigne

le verger

faire la moisson

le pommier

la meule de foin

cueillir

le blé

le tracteur

semer

labourer

le verger	orchard
le pommier	apple tree
cueillir	to pick
le tracteur	tractor
labourer	to plough
l'épouvantail(m)	scarecrow

l'épouvantail

65

At work

aller travailler

être en retard

arriver à l'heure

l'heure du déjeuner

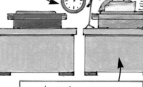

les heures supplémentaires

aller travailler	to go to work	**l'heure(f) du déjeuner**	lunch hour
être en retard	to be late	**les heures supplémentaires**	overtime
arriver à l'heure	to be on time		

le bureau

engager quelqu'un

travailleuses

prendre sa retraite

la patronne

la secrétaire

l'employé

paresseux

renvoyer quelqu'un

le bureau	office	**l'employé(m)**	employee (m)
la patronne	boss (f)	**travailleur (travailleuse)**	hard-working
la secrétaire	secretary (f)	**paresseux (paresseuse)**	lazy
engager quelqu'un	to employ someone	**prendre sa retraite**	to retire
		renvoyer quelqu'un	to fire someone

le métier

le plombier

l'ouvrier

l'architecte

le métier	job, profession
l'ouvrier(m)	builder, labourer (m)
le plombier	plumber (m/f)
l'architecte(m)	architect (m/f)

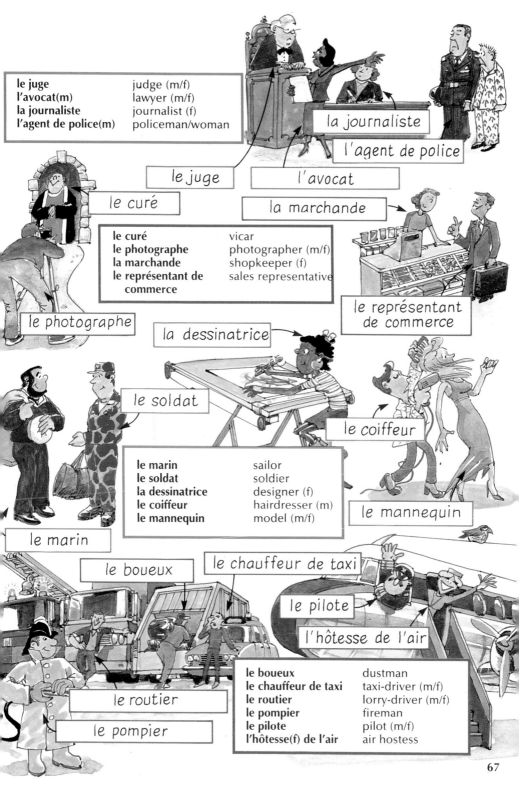

le juge	judge (m/f)
l'avocat(m)	lawyer (m/f)
la journaliste	journalist (f)
l'agent de police(m)	policeman/woman

la journaliste

l'agent de police

le juge

l'avocat

le curé

la marchande

le curé	vicar
le photographe	photographer (m/f)
la marchande	shopkeeper (f)
le représentant de commerce	sales representative

le représentant de commerce

le photographe

la dessinatrice

le soldat

le coiffeur

le marin	sailor
le soldat	soldier
la dessinatrice	designer (f)
le coiffeur	hairdresser (m)
le mannequin	model (m/f)

le mannequin

le marin

le boueux

le chauffeur de taxi

le pilote

l'hôtesse de l'air

le routier

le pompier

le boueux	dustman
le chauffeur de taxi	taxi-driver (m/f)
le routier	lorry-driver (m/f)
le pompier	fireman
le pilote	pilot (m/f)
l'hôtesse(f) de l'air	air hostess

Illness and health

se sentir malade

prendre la température

le thermomètre

avoir de la fièvre

le médecin

l'ordonnance

guérir

se sentir mieux

le comprimé

en bonne santé

se sentir malade	to feel ill	**le médecin**	doctor (m/f)
prendre la température	to take someone's temperature	**l'ordonnance**(f)	prescription
le thermomètre	thermometer	**guérir**	to cure
avoir de la fièvre	to have a temperature	**le comprimé**	pill
		se sentir mieux	to feel better
		en bonne santé	healthy

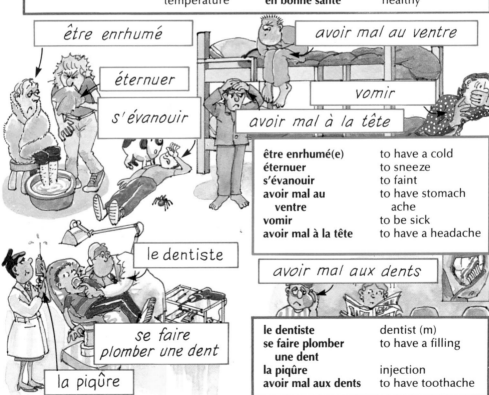

être enrhumé

éternuer

s'évanouir

avoir mal au ventre

vomir

avoir mal à la tête

être enrhumé(e)	to have a cold
éternuer	to sneeze
s'évanouir	to faint
avoir mal au ventre	to have stomach ache
vomir	to be sick
avoir mal à la tête	to have a headache

le dentiste

se faire plomber une dent

la piqûre

avoir mal aux dents

le dentiste	dentist (m)
se faire plomber une dent	to have a filling
la piqûre	injection
avoir mal aux dents	to have toothache

l'hôpital(m)	hospital	la blessure	cut, wound
le service des urgences	casualty department	la brûlure	burn
se casser la jambe	to break your leg	se fouler le poignet	to sprain your wrist
le bleu	bruise	le sparadrap	sticking plaster
		le bandage	bandage

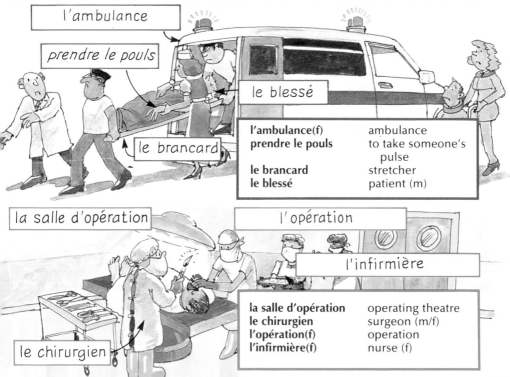

l'ambulance(f)	ambulance
prendre le pouls	to take someone's pulse
le brancard	stretcher
le blessé	patient (m)

la salle d'opération	operating theatre
le chirurgien	surgeon (m/f)
l'opération(f)	operation
l'infirmière(f)	nurse (f)

School and education

l'école maternelle
l'école primaire
le directeur
le collège
la directrice
l'université

l'école(f) maternelle	nursery school	**le collège**	secondary school
l'école primaire	primary school	**la directrice**	headmistress
le directeur	headmaster	**l'université(f)**	university

au collège
la salle de classe
le cours
le professeur
la carte
enseigner
l'élève
le tableau noir
apprendre
facile
difficile
la craie
poser une question
lire
écrire

au collège	at school	**facile**	easy
la salle de classe	classroom	**difficile**	difficult
la carte	map	**le tableau noir**	blackboard
le cours	lesson	**la craie**	chalk
le professeur	teacher (m/f)	**lire**	to read
enseigner	to teach	**écrire**	to write
l'élève (m/f)	pupil (m/f)	**poser une question**	to ask a question
apprendre	to learn		

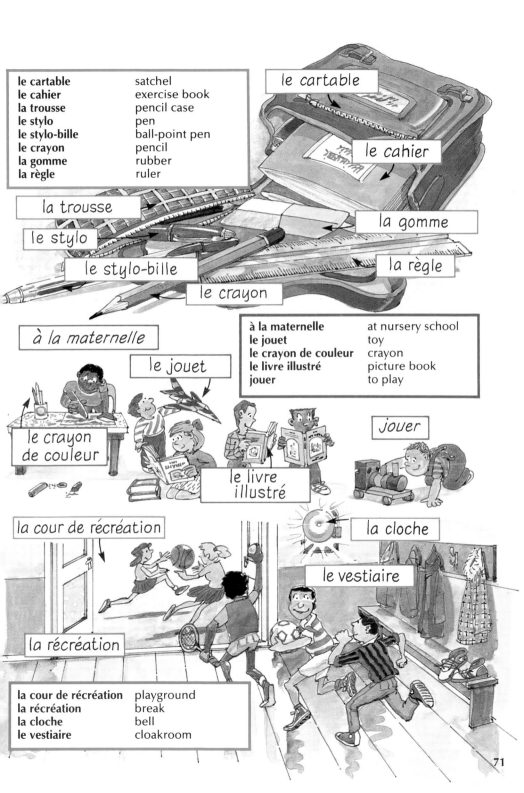

le cartable	satchel
le cahier	exercise book
la trousse	pencil case
le stylo	pen
le stylo-bille	ball-point pen
le crayon	pencil
la gomme	rubber
la règle	ruler

le cartable

le cahier

la trousse

la gomme

le stylo

la règle

le stylo-bille

le crayon

à la maternelle

à la maternelle	at nursery school
le jouet	toy
le crayon de couleur	crayon
le livre illustré	picture book
jouer	to play

le jouet

le crayon de couleur

jouer

le livre illustré

la cour de récréation

la cloche

le vestiaire

la récréation

la cour de récréation	playground
la récréation	break
la cloche	bell
le vestiaire	cloakroom

School and education

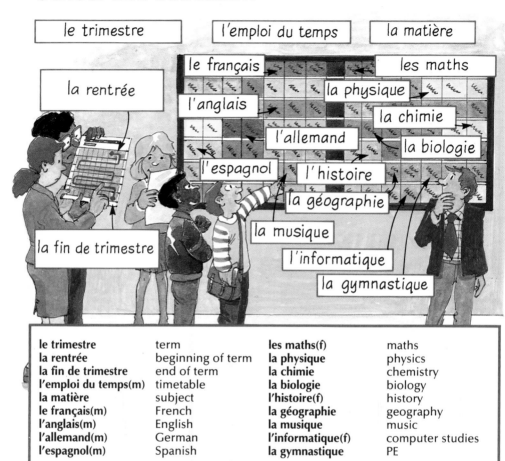

| le trimestre | la rentrée | la fin de trimestre | l'emploi du temps | la matière | le français | l'anglais | l'allemand | l'espagnol | les maths | la physique | la chimie | la biologie | l'histoire | la géographie | la musique | l'informatique | la gymnastique |

le trimestre	term	**les maths(f)**	maths
la rentrée	beginning of term	**la physique**	physics
la fin de trimestre	end of term	**la chimie**	chemistry
l'emploi du temps(m)	timetable	**la biologie**	biology
la matière	subject	**l'histoire(f)**	history
le français(m)	French	**la géographie**	geography
l'anglais(m)	English	**la musique**	music
l'allemand(m)	German	**l'informatique(f)**	computer studies
l'espagnol(m)	Spanish	**la gymnastique**	PE

A B C D E F G H I J K L M N O P Q R S T U V W X Y Z

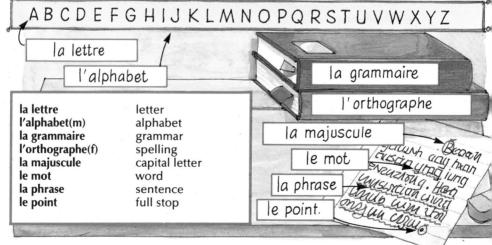

| la lettre | l'alphabet | la grammaire | l'orthographe | la majuscule | le mot | la phrase | le point. |

la lettre	letter
l'alphabet(m)	alphabet
la grammaire	grammar
l'orthographe(f)	spelling
la majuscule	capital letter
le mot	word
la phrase	sentence
le point	full stop

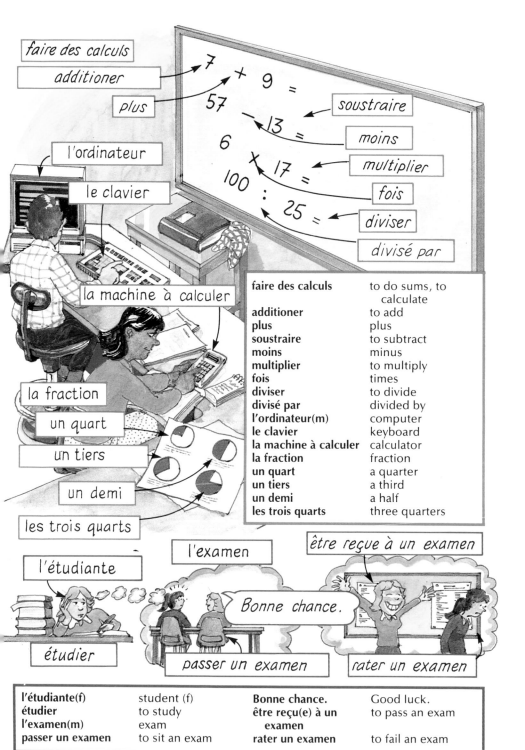

faire des calculs

additioner

plus

7 + 9 =

57 − 13 =

6 × 17 =

100 : 25 =

soustraire

moins

multiplier

fois

diviser

divisé par

l'ordinateur

le clavier

la machine à calculer

la fraction

un quart

un tiers

un demi

les trois quarts

faire des calculs	to do sums, to calculate
additioner	to add
plus	plus
soustraire	to subtract
moins	minus
multiplier	to multiply
fois	times
diviser	to divide
divisé par	divided by
l'ordinateur(m)	computer
le clavier	keyboard
la machine à calculer	calculator
la fraction	fraction
un quart	a quarter
un tiers	a third
un demi	a half
les trois quarts	three quarters

l'examen

être reçue à un examen

l'étudiante

Bonne chance.

étudier

passer un examen

rater un examen

l'étudiante(f)	student (f)	Bonne chance.	Good luck.
étudier	to study	être reçu(e) à un examen	to pass an exam
l'examen(m)	exam		
passer un examen	to sit an exam	rater un examen	to fail an exam

73

Shapes and sizes

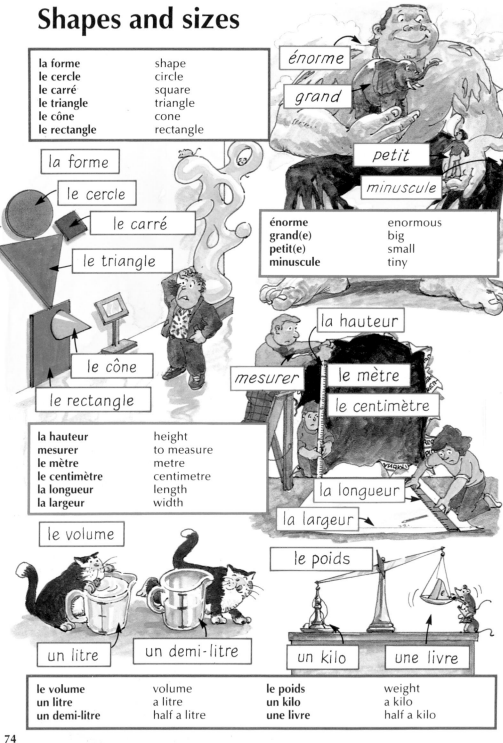

la forme	shape
le cercle	circle
le carré	square
le triangle	triangle
le cône	cone
le rectangle	rectangle

énorme

grand

petit

minuscule

énorme	enormous
grand(e)	big
petit(e)	small
minuscule	tiny

la forme

le cercle

le carré

le triangle

le cône

le rectangle

la hauteur

mesurer

le mètre

le centimètre

la longueur

la largeur

la hauteur	height
mesurer	to measure
le mètre	metre
le centimètre	centimetre
la longueur	length
la largeur	width

le volume

le poids

un litre

un demi-litre

un kilo

une livre

le volume	volume		**le poids**	weight
un litre	a litre		**un kilo**	a kilo
un demi-litre	half a litre		**une livre**	half a kilo

Numbers

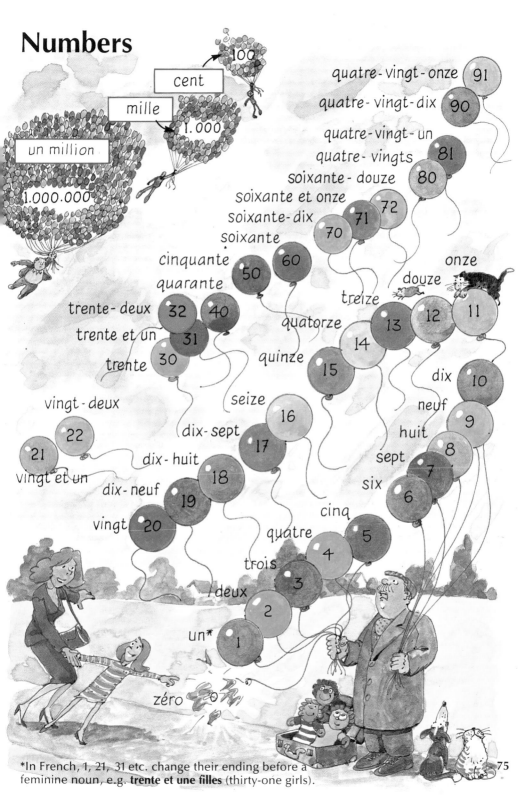

cent — 100

mille — 1.000

un million — 1.000.000

quatre-vingt-onze 91
quatre-vingt-dix 90
quatre-vingt-un
quatre-vingts 81
soixante-douze 80
soixante et onze
soixante-dix 72
soixante 71
70

onze
douze
cinquante 60
quarante 50
treize
trente-deux 40 quatorze
trente et un 32 13 12 11
trente 31 quinze 14
30 15

seize dix 10
vingt-deux 16 neuf 9
22 dix-sept huit 8
21 17 sept 7
vingt et un dix-huit six 6
dix-neuf 18
vingt 19 cinq 5
20 quatre 4
trois
deux 3
2
un* 1
zéro 0

*In French, 1, 21, 31 etc. change their ending before a
feminine noun, e.g. **trente et une filles** (thirty-one girls).

75

Sport

être en forme

faire du jogging

le bandeau

faire du keepfit

les tennis

le survêtement

être en forme	to be fit	**le bandeau**	headband
faire du keepfit	to exercise	**les tennis(m)**	tennis shoes
faire du jogging	to jog	**le survêtement**	tracksuit

jouer au tennis

faire du golf

le club de golf

le court de tennis

jouer au squash

le joueur

In.

servir

Out.

le filet

la balle

la raquette

jouer au tennis	to play tennis	**le filet**	net
le court de tennis	tennis court	**la balle**	ball
le joueur	player (m)	**la raquette**	racket
servir	to serve	**faire du golf**	to play golf
In.	In.	**le club de golf**	golf club
Out.	Out.	**jouer au squash**	to play squash

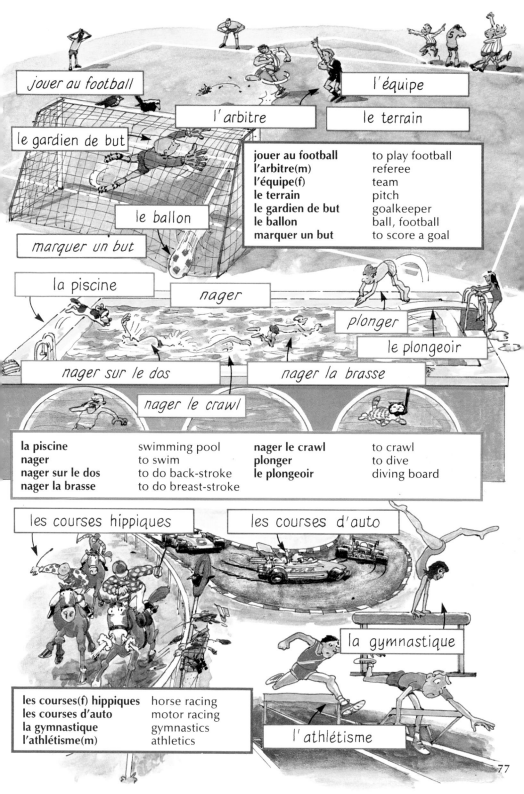

jouer au football

l'équipe

l'arbitre

le terrain

le gardien de but

jouer au football	to play football
l'arbitre(m)	referee
l'équipe(f)	team
le terrain	pitch
le gardien de but	goalkeeper
le ballon	ball, football
marquer un but	to score a goal

le ballon

marquer un but

la piscine

nager

plonger

le plongeoir

nager sur le dos

nager la brasse

nager le crawl

la piscine	swimming pool	**nager le crawl**	to crawl
nager	to swim	**plonger**	to dive
nager sur le dos	to do back-stroke	**le plongeoir**	diving board
nager la brasse	to do breast-stroke		

les courses hippiques

les courses d'auto

la gymnastique

les courses(f) hippiques	horse racing
les courses d'auto	motor racing
la gymnastique	gymnastics
l'athlétisme(m)	athletics

l'athlétisme

77

Celebrations

l'anniversaire(m)	birthday
la fête	party
le ballon	balloon
Bon anniversaire.	Happy birthday.
inviter	to invite
bien s'amuser	to have fun, to enjoy yourself
le gâteau	cake
la bougie	candle
la carte d'anniversaire	birthday card
le cadeau	present
l'emballage(m)	wrapping

l'anniversaire

la fête

le ballon

Bon anniversaire.

inviter

bien s'amuser

le gâteau

la bougie

le cadeau

l'emballage

la carte d'anniversaire

la veille de Noël

Pâques

Noël

le jour de Noël

le sapin de Noël

Pâques	Easter
Noël	Christmas
la veille de Noël	Christmas Eve
le jour de Noël	Christmas Day
le sapin de Noël	Christmas tree

se fiancer	to get engaged
les noces(f)	wedding
se marier	to get married
le marié	bridegroom
la mariée	bride
l'invité(m)	guest (m)
féliciter	to congratulate
le bouquet	bouquet
être heureux (heureuse)	to be happy
le voyage de noces	honeymoon

se fiancer

les noces

se marier

le marié

la mariée

l'invité

féliciter

le bouquet

être heureux

le voyage de noces

Joyeux Noël.	Happy Christmas.
le chant de Noël	Christmas carol
offrir	to give (a present)
recevoir	to receive
Merci beaucoup.	Thank you very much.
remercier	to thank

Joyeux Noël.

le chant de Noël

offrir

recevoir

Merci beaucoup.

remercier

le Réveillon

le jour de l'An

célébrer

Bonne année.

le Réveillon	New Year's Eve
le jour de l'An	New Year's Day
célébrer	to celebrate
Bonne année.	Happy New Year.

Days and dates

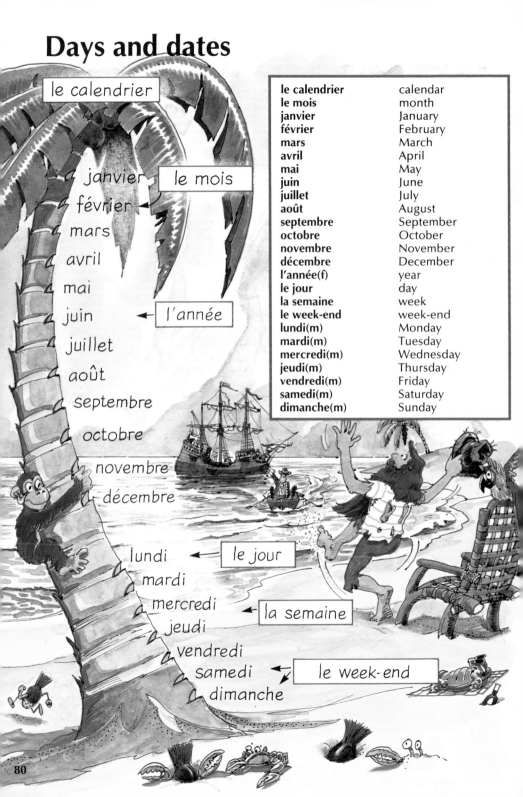

le calendrier

le mois

janvier
février
mars
avril
mai
juin
juillet
août
septembre
octobre
novembre
décembre

l'année

le calendrier	calendar
le mois	month
janvier	January
février	February
mars	March
avril	April
mai	May
juin	June
juillet	July
août	August
septembre	September
octobre	October
novembre	November
décembre	December
l'année(f)	year
le jour	day
la semaine	week
le week-end	week-end
lundi(m)	Monday
mardi(m)	Tuesday
mercredi(m)	Wednesday
jeudi(m)	Thursday
vendredi(m)	Friday
samedi(m)	Saturday
dimanche(m)	Sunday

lundi
mardi
mercredi
jeudi
vendredi
samedi
dimanche

le jour

la semaine

le week-end

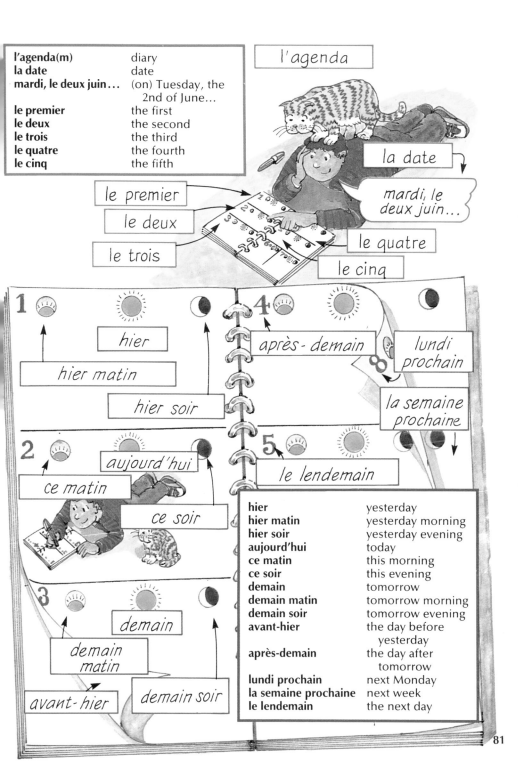

l'agenda(m)	diary
la date	date
mardi, le deux juin...	(on) Tuesday, the 2nd of June...
le premier	the first
le deux	the second
le trois	the third
le quatre	the fourth
le cinq	the fifth

l'agenda

la date

mardi, le deux juin...

le premier

le deux

le trois

le quatre

le cinq

1 hier

hier matin

hier soir

4 après-demain

lundi prochain

la semaine prochaine

2 aujourd'hui

ce matin

ce soir

5 le lendemain

3 demain

demain matin

avant-hier

demain soir

hier	yesterday
hier matin	yesterday morning
hier soir	yesterday evening
aujourd'hui	today
ce matin	this morning
ce soir	this evening
demain	tomorrow
demain matin	tomorrow morning
demain soir	tomorrow evening
avant-hier	the day before yesterday
après-demain	the day after tomorrow
lundi prochain	next Monday
la semaine prochaine	next week
le lendemain	the next day

Time

l'aube

le lever du soleil

Il commence à faire jour.

le matin

le soleil

le ciel

Il fait jour.

le jour

l'aube(f)	dawn	**le soleil**	sun
le lever du soleil	sunrise	**le ciel**	sky
Il commence à faire jour.	It is getting light.	**Il fait jour.**	It is light.
le matin	morning, in the morning	**le jour**	day, in the daytime

l'après-midi

le soir

le coucher du soleil

La nuit tombe.

la nuit

les étoiles

la lune

Il fait nuit.

l'après-midi(m or f)	afternoon, in the afternoon	**La nuit tombe.**	It is getting dark.
		la nuit	night, at night
le soir	evening, in the evening	**les étoiles(f)**	stars
		la lune	moon
le coucher du soleil	sunset	**Il fait nuit.**	It is dark.

Quelle heure est-il?	What time is it?	**dix heures moins le quart**	a quarter to 10
l'heure(f)	hour		
la minute	minute	**dix heures cinq**	five past 10
la seconde	second	**dix heures et quart**	a quarter past 10
Il est une heure.	It is 1 o'clock.	**dix heures et demie**	half past 10
Il est trois heures.	It is 3 o'clock.	**huit heures du matin**	8 a.m.
midi	midday	**huit heures du soir**	8 p.m.
minuit	midnight		

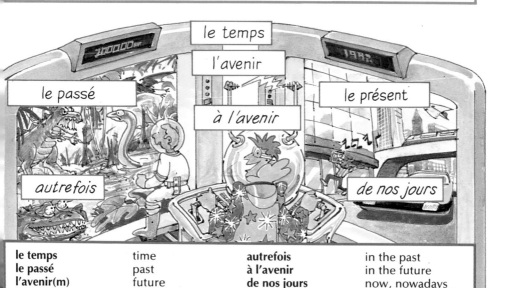

le temps	time	**autrefois**	in the past
le passé	past	**à l'avenir**	in the future
l'avenir(m)	future	**de nos jours**	now, nowadays
le présent	present		

Weather and seasons

la saison	season
le printemps	spring
l'été(f)	summer
l'automne(m)	autumn
l'hiver(m)	winter

la saison

le printemps

le temps

Il pleut.

l'hiver

la pluie

l'orage

le nuage

l'automne

l'été

la foudre

le tonnerre

l'arc-en-ciel

le parapluie

trempé jusqu'aux os

les bottes de caoutchouc

la flaque d'eau

la goutte de pluie

la grêle

l'inondation

le temps	weather
Il pleut.	It's raining.
la pluie	rain
l'orage(m)	thunder storm
le nuage	cloud
la foudre	lightning
le tonnerre	thunder
le parapluie	umbrella
l'arc-en-ciel(m)	rainbow
les bottes(f) de caoutchouc	wellington boots
trempé(e) jusqu'aux os	soaked to the skin
la flaque d'eau	puddle
la goutte de pluie	raindrop
la grêle	hail
l'inondation(f)	flood

le climat — climate
la météo — weather forecast
Quel temps fait-il? — What is the weather like?

le climat

la météo

Quel temps fait-il ?

Il fait beau.

Le soleil brille.

transpirer

J'ai chaud.

Il fait beau. — It's fine.
Le soleil brille. — The sun is shining.
transpirer — to sweat
J'ai chaud. — I'm hot.

le vent

Il fait du vent.

le vent — wind
Il fait du vent. — It's windy.
le brouillard — fog
Il fait du brouillard. — It's foggy.

Il fait froid

la neige

le brouillard

Il fait du brouillard.

être gelée

le gel

le bonhomme de neige

le glaçon

Il neige.

fondre

Il fait froid. — It's cold.
être gelé(e) — to be frozen
le gel — frost
le glaçon — icicle
la neige — snow
le bonhomme de neige — snowman
Il neige. — It's snowing.
fondre — to thaw

World and universe

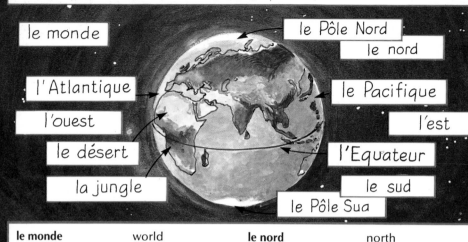

le monde

le Pôle Nord

le nord

l'Atlantique

le Pacifique

l'ouest

l'est

le désert

l'Equateur

la jungle

le sud

le Pôle Sua

le monde	world	**le nord**	north
l'Atlantique(m)	Atlantic Ocean	**le Pacifique**	Pacific Ocean
l'ouest(m)	west	**l'est(m)**	east
le désert	desert	**l'Equateur(m)**	Equator
la jungle	jungle	**le sud**	south
le Pôle Nord	North Pole	**le Pôle Sud**	South Pole

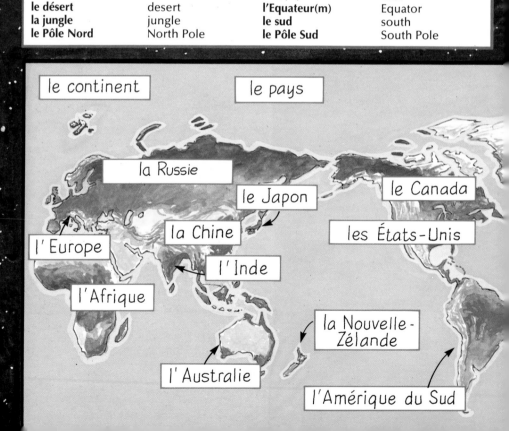

le continent

le pays

la Russie

le Japon

le Canada

la Chine

les États-Unis

l'Europe

l'Inde

l'Afrique

la Nouvelle-Zélande

l'Australie

l'Amérique du Sud

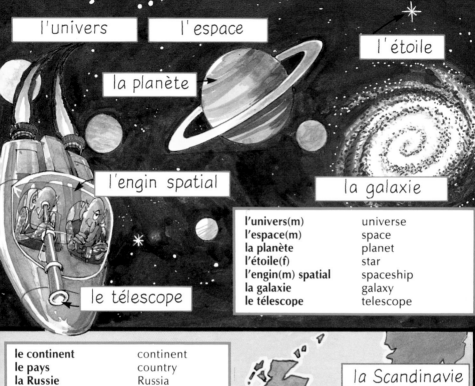

l'univers

l'espace

l'étoile

la planète

l'engin spatial

la galaxie

le télescope

l'univers(m)	universe
l'espace(m)	space
la planète	planet
l'étoile(f)	star
l'engin(m) spatial	spaceship
la galaxie	galaxy
le télescope	telescope

le continent	continent
le pays	country
la Russie	Russia
l'Europe(f)	Europe
l'Afrique(f)	Africa
le Japon	Japan
la Chine	China
l'Inde(f)	India
l'Australie(f)	Australia
la Nouvelle-Zélande	New Zealand
le Canada	Canada
les Etats-Unis(m)	United States
l'Amérique(f) du Sud	South America

la Scandinavie	Scandinavia
la Grande-Bretagne	Great Britain
les Pays-Bas(m)	Netherlands
la Belgique	Belgium
l'Allemagne(f)	Germany
la France	France
la Suisse	Switzerland
l'Italie(f)	Italy
l'Espagne(f)	Spain

la Scandinavie

la Grande-Bretagne

les Pays-Bas

la Belgique

l'Allemagne

la France

la Suisse

l'Italie

l'Espagne

Politics

le président

le parlement

le député

le premier ministre

le gouvernement

le président	president (m/f)
le parlement	parliament
le député	member of parliament (m/f)
le premier ministre	prime minister (m/f)
le gouvernement	government

le parti

le chef

populaire

le membre

le parti	party
le chef	leader (m/f)
populaire	popular
le membre	member (m/f)

l'élection

voter

la gauche

le centre

la droite

s'inscrire à

être membre de

gagner

perdre

l'élection(f)	election	**le centre**	centre
voter	to vote	**la droite**	right, right wing
gagner	to win	**s'inscrire à**	to join
perdre	to lose	**être membre de**	to belong to
la gauche	left, left wing		

les medias(m)	the media
interviewer	to interview
important(e)	important
intéressant(e)	interesting
le journal	newspaper
les informations(f)	news
le gros titre	headline
l'article(m)	article
vrai(e)	true
faux (fausse)	false

les medias

interviewer

important

intéressant

le journal

les informations

le gros titre

l'article

vrai

faux

la politique

le salaire

les impôts

la société

démocratique

le syndicat

le chômage

la politique	politics		**les impôts(m)**	taxes
la société	society		**le syndicat**	trade union
démocratique	democratic		**le chômage**	unemployment
le salaire	salary, wages			

Describing things

bruyant

calme

obéissant

pareilles

méchant

bruyant(e)	noisy
calme	quiet, calm
obéissant(e)	obedient
méchant(e)	naughty
pareil(le)	same
différent(e)	different

différentes

ensemble

seul

occupé

utile

effrayé

occupé(e)	busy
utile	useful
ensemble	together
seul(e)	alone
effrayé(e)	frightened
courageux	brave, courageous
(courageuse)	

courageux

négligent

fâchée

plein d'entrain

soigneux

contente de

ennuyeux

négligent(e)	careless
soigneux (soigneuse)	careful
fâché(e)	cross
content(e) de	pleased with
plein(e) d'entrain	lively
ennuyeux	boring
(ennuyeuse)	

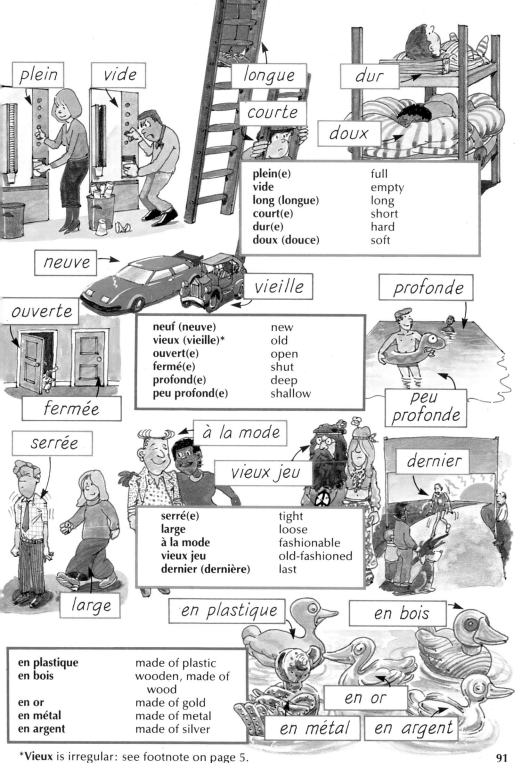

plein

vide

longue

courte

dur

doux

plein(e)	full
vide	empty
long (longue)	long
court(e)	short
dur(e)	hard
doux (douce)	soft

neuve

vieille

ouverte

profonde

neuf (neuve)	new
vieux (vieille)*	old
ouvert(e)	open
fermé(e)	shut
profond(e)	deep
peu profond(e)	shallow

fermée

peu profonde

serrée

à la mode

vieux jeu

dernier

serré(e)	tight
large	loose
à la mode	fashionable
vieux jeu	old-fashioned
dernier (dernière)	last

large

en plastique

en bois

en or

en métal

en argent

en plastique	made of plastic
en bois	wooden, made of wood
en or	made of gold
en métal	made of metal
en argent	made of silver

*****Vieux** is irregular: see footnote on page 5.

Colours

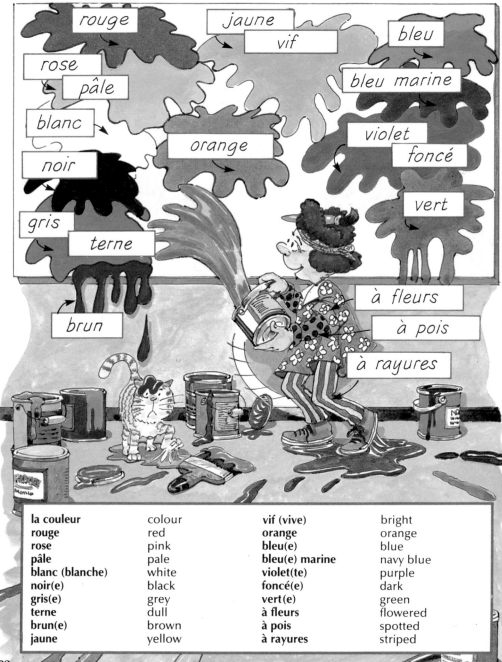

la couleur

rouge

jaune
vif

bleu

rose
pâle

bleu marine

blanc

orange

violet
foncé

noir

vert

gris
terne

à fleurs

à pois

à rayures

brun

la couleur	colour	**vif (vive)**	bright
rouge	red	**orange**	orange
rose	pink	**bleu(e)**	blue
pâle	pale	**bleu(e) marine**	navy blue
blanc (blanche)	white	**violet(te)**	purple
noir(e)	black	**foncé(e)**	dark
gris(e)	grey	**vert(e)**	green
terne	dull	**à fleurs**	flowered
brun(e)	brown	**à pois**	spotted
jaune	yellow	**à rayures**	striped

In, on, under...

dans	in	**contre**	against
sur	on	**à travers**	through
sous	under	**parmi**	among
par dessus	over	**vers**	to, towards
dans	into	**de** (e.g. s'échapper	away from (e.g.to
hors de	out of	de)	run away from)
à côté de	beside	**en haut**	up
entre	between	**en bas**	down
près de	near	**en face de**	opposite
loin de	far away from	**avec**	with
devant	in front of	**sans**	without
derrière	behind		

Action words

chuchoter

crier

chercher

attendre

s'appuyer sur

tenir

chuchoter	to whisper
crier	to shout
chercher	to look for
attendre	to wait for
s'appuyer sur	to lean on
tenir	to hold

porter

ramasser

laisser tomber

déposer

| porter | to carry | ramasser | to pick up |
| laisser tomber | to drop | déposer | to put down |

toucher

fermer

ouvrir

verser

remplir

agiter

vider

toucher	to touch
ouvrir	to open
fermer	to close
verser	to pour
remplir	to fill
agiter	to shake
vider	to empty

déchirer

lancer

attraper

déchirer	to tear
raccommoder	to mend
lancer	to throw
attraper	to catch
renverser	to knock over
casser	to break

raccommoder

renverser

casser

voler

glisser

tirer

pousser

s'échapper

suivre

se cacher

tirer	to pull	**s'échapper**	to run away
pousser	to push	**suivre**	to follow
voler	to steal	**se cacher**	to hide
glisser	to slip		

Grammar hints

In order to speak French well, you need to learn a bit about the grammar, that is, how you put words together and make sentences. On the next few pages there are some hints on French grammar. Don't worry if you cannot remember them all at first. Try to learn a little grammar at a time and then practise using it.

Nouns

In French all nouns are either masculine or feminine. The word you use for "the" is **le** before a masculine noun, **la** before a feminine noun and **l'** before nouns beginning with a vowel:

le chapeau	the hat
la jupe	the skirt
l'imperméable (m)	the raincoat
l'écharpe (f)	the scarf

Some nouns have a masculine and a feminine form. These are often nouns which describe what people are or what they do:

l'étudiant	the student (m)
l'étudiante	the student (f)
le boulanger	the baker (m)
la boulangère	the baker (f)

When they appear in the illustrated section, only the form which matches the picture is given, but both masculine and feminine forms are given in the word list at the back.

Plurals

When you are talking about more than one thing, the word for "the" is always **les:**

les chapeaux	the hats
les jupes	
les imperméables	
les écharpes	

You add "s" to most nouns to make the plural, but it is not pronounced.

Some plurals are formed differently. Nouns ending in "au" and "eu" all add "x" in the plural:

le bateau	the boat
les bateaux	
le jeu	the game
les jeux	

Nouns ending in "al" change the "al" to "aux" in the plural:

le cheval	the horse
les chevaux	

a, an and some

The word for "a" is **un** before a masculine noun and **une** before a feminine noun:

un chapeau
une jupe
un imperméable
une écharpe

The word for "some" or "any" is **du** before a masculine noun, **de la** before a feminine noun and **de l'** before nouns beginning with a vowel. **Des** is used before plurals.

The French often say "some" where there is nothing in English:

Elle mange du poisson. She is eating fish.

After a negative, **de** is used on its own:

Je ne mange jamais de riz. I never eat rice.

this, that

"This" or "that" is **ce** before a masculine noun, **cette** before a feminine noun and **cet** before a masculine noun beginning with a vowel. The plural, meaning "these" or "those", is **ces**:

ce chapeau	**cette jupe**
ces chapeaux	**ces jupes**

my, your

"My", "your", "his", "her" and so on are called possessive adjectives. In French they change according to whether the noun which follows is masculine or feminine, singular or plural:

(m)	(f)	(pl)
my		
mon gilet	**ma jupe**	**mes gants**
my cardigan	my skirt	my gloves
your		
ton gilet	**ta jupe**	**tes gants**
his/her		
son gilet	**sa jupe**	**ses gants**
our		
notre gilet	**notre jupe**	**nos gants**

your		
votre gilet	**votre jupe**	**vos gants**
their		
leur gilet	**leur jupe**	**leurs gants**

With nouns which begin with a vowel, you always use the masculine form of the possessive adjective:

mon imperméable (m)
mon écharpe (f)

Adjectives

Adjectives are describing words. In French, adjectives change their endings depending on whether they are describing a masculine or a feminine word and whether it is singular or plural. You usually add an "e" to the masculine form of the adjective to make it feminine, unless it already ends in an "e":

Il est grand. He is tall.
Elle est grande. She is tall.

To make an adjective plural, you usually add an "s":

Ils sont grands. They (m) are tall.
Elles sont grandes. They (f) are tall.

However, adjectives ending in "au" add an "x":

beau	beautiful
beaux	

and adjectives ending in "al" change to "aux":

égal	equal
égaux	

Some adjectives do not simply add "e" in the feminine:

beau (m) belle (f)   beautiful
bon (m) bonne (f)   good
nouveau (m) nouvelle (f)   new

When these appear in the illustrated section, the form which matches the picture is given. However it is useful to learn both the masculine and feminine forms, so both are given in the word box and in the word list at the back.

In French, adjectives usually come after a noun:

un blouson rouge   a red jacket
du lait chaud   hot milk

However these common adjectives usually come before the noun:

autre	other
beau	beautiful
bon	good
gentil	nice
grand	big, tall
gros	fat, big
jeune	young
joli	pretty
long	long
mauvais	bad
petit	small
vaste	huge
vieux	old

Comparing adjectives

To compare things you put **plus...que** (more...than), **aussi...que** (as...as) and **le/la plus** (the most) with an adjective. The adjective agrees in the usual way.

Elle est plus grande que son frère. She is taller than her brother.
Elle est plus grande. She is taller.
Son frère est aussi grand que moi. Her brother is as tall as me.
Elle est la plus grande. She is the tallest.

Some common adjectives do not add **plus** or **le plus,** but change completely:

bon	good
meilleur	better
le meilleur	the best
mauvais	bad
pire	worse
le pire	the worst

Pronouns

"I", "you", "he", "she" and so on are called pronouns. You use them in place of a noun:

je	I	**nous**	we
tu	you	**vous**	you
il	he/it	**ils**	they (m)
elle	she/it	**elles**	they (f)

In French there are two words for "you": **tu** and **vous**. You say **tu** to a friend and **vous** when you want to be polite or don't know someone very well, or when you are talking to more than one person. "It" is **il** for a masculine word and **elle** for a feminine word. "They" is **ils** for masculine words and **elles** for feminine words. For masculine and feminine things together, you use **ils**.

Verbs

French verbs (action words) change their endings according to who is doing the action. Most of them follow regular patterns of endings. There are three main patterns according to whether the verb's infinitive (e.g. in English: "to dance"; "to do") ends in "er", "ir" or "re". These are the endings for the present tense:

danser   to dance

je danse   I dance, I am dancing
tu danses
il/elle danse
nous dansons
vous dansez
ils/elles dansent

choisir   to choose

je choisis
tu choisis
il/elle choisit
nous choisissons
nous choisissez
ils/elles choisissent

attendre   to wait

j'attends
tu attends
il/elle attend
nous attendons
vous attendez
ils/elles attendent

Some of the most common verbs, such as **avoir** (to have) and **être** (to be), do not follow any of these patterns and you need to learn them separately. They are known as irregular verbs. The present tense of **avoir** and **être** are shown below. You can find the present tense of other irregular verbs on page 102.

avoir	être
j'ai	je suis
tu as	tu es
il/elle a	il/elle est
nous avons	nous sommes
vous avez	vous êtes
ils/elles ont	ils/elles sont

The future tense is used for things you are going to do (in English, "I will dance" or "I am going to dance"). In French the future tense is made by adding these endings to the infinitive:

danser	choisir
je danser ai	je choisir ai
tu danser as	tu choisir as
il/elle danser a	il/elle choisir a
nous danser ons	nous choisir ons
vous danser ez	vous choisir ez
ils/elles danser ont	ils/elles choisir ont

For "re" verbs, the "e" is left off the infinitive before the endings are added:

j'attendr ai
tu attendr as
il/elle attendr a
nous attendr ons
vous attendr ez
ils/elles attendr ont

For events which have already happened ("I have danced" or "I danced"), you use the perfect tense. You make the perfect by putting the present of **avoir** with the past participle of the verb. The past participle is based on the infinitive and varies according to whether the verb is an "er", "ir" or "re" type:

infinitive	past participle
danser	dansé
choisir	choisi
attendre	attendu

Here are the perfect tenses of **danser, choisir** and **attendre:**

j'ai dansé
tu as dansé
il/elle a dansé
nous avons dansé
vous avez dansé
ils/elles ont dansé

j'ai choisi
tu as choisi
il/elle a choisi
nous avons choisi
vous avez choisi
ils/elles ont choisi

j'ai attendu
tu as attendu
il/elle a attendu
nous avons attendu
vous avez attendu
ils/elles ont attendu

The following common French verbs use **être** instead of **avoir** to make the perfect tense:

aller	to go
arriver	to arrive
descendre	to go down
devenir	to become
entrer	to go in
monter	to go up
mourir	to die
naître	to be born
partir	to leave
rentrer	to come back
retourner	to go back
rester	to stay
sortir	to go out
tomber	to fall
venir	to come

When you make the perfect tense with **être,** the past participle changes according to whether the subject of the verb is masculine or feminine, singular or plural, like an adjective:

je suis allé(e)	nous sommes allé(e)s
tu es allé(e)	vous êtes allé(e)(s)
il est allé	ils sont allés
elle est allée	elles sont allées

You add the "e" or "s" if the subject is feminine or plural.

Reflexive verbs

Verbs which have **se** before the infinitive are called reflexive verbs. These verbs usually involve doing something to yourself.

se laver	to wash oneself
s'amuser	to enjoy oneself
se coucher	to go to bed

Se means "self" and changes according to who is doing the action:

je me couche   I am going to bed
tu te couches   you are going to bed
il/elle se couche
nous nous couchons
vous vous couchez
ils/elles se couchent

You always use **être** to make the perfect tense of reflexive verbs:

je me suis couché(e)
tu t'es couché(e)
il s'est couché
elle s'est couchée
nous nous sommes couché(e)s
vous vous êtes couché(e)s
ils se sont couchés
elles se sont couchées

Negatives

To make a negative in French you put **ne** (or **n'** in front of a vowel) and **pas** around the verb:

Je n'aime pas les chiens. I do not like dogs.
Je ne sortirai pas. I will not go out.

In the perfect tense the **ne** and **pas** go round **avoir** or **être**:

Je n'ai pas fini. I have not finished.
Je ne suis pas allé au cinéma. I did not go to the cinema.

With reflexive verbs you put the **ne** before the reflexive pronoun (**me, te, se** etc):

Je ne me couche pas tard. I do not go to bed late.
Je ne me suis pas lavé ce matin. I have not washed this morning.

Object pronouns

An object pronoun is one which you put in place of a noun that is the object of a verb:

Il cherche ses clés. He is looking for his keys.
Il les cherche. He is looking for them.

These are the object pronouns:

me	me	**nous**	us
te	you	**vous**	you
le	him/it	**les**	them
la	her/it		

In French you put the object pronoun just before the verb:

Je le regarde. I am looking at him.
Il ne me regarde pas. He is not looking at me.

In the perfect tense you put the object pronoun before **avoir** or **être** and the past participle changes like an adjective according to whether the pronoun is masculine, feminine, singular or plural:

Je l'ai regardé. I looked at him.
Je l'ai regardée. I looked at her.
Les clés! Je les ai trouvées. The keys! I've found them.

Questions

A common way to make a question in French is using the phrase **est-ce que:**

Est-ce que tu as des soeurs? Have you any sisters?
Est-ce que Jean vient avec nous? Is Jean coming with us?
Est-ce qu'il y a une pharmacie par ici? Is there a chemist's around here?

Below are some questions beginning with useful question words.
When you use these, you put the subject after the verb; if the subject is a pronoun, you put a hyphen between them:

Qui est ce monsieur? Who is this man?
Que fais-tu? What are you doing?
Quand est-elle allée à Paris? When did she go to Paris?
Comment es-tu venu? How did you get here?
Combien coûte le billet? How much does the ticket cost?
Combien de temps dure le film? How long is the film?
Combien de frères as-tu? How many brothers do you have?
Pourquoi a-t-il* dit cela? Why did he say that?
Où est le cinéma? Where is the cinema?
D'où venez-vous? Where are you from?

Quel means "which" or "what" and changes like an adjective to agree with the noun which follows:

Quel temps fait-il? What's the weather like?
Quelle heure est-il? What time is it?
Quels livres? Which books?
Quelles langues parles-tu? Which languages do you speak?

Irregular verbs

Here are the present tenses of some common irregular verbs, together with the **je** form of the future and perfect tenses. Try to learn these verbs, one or two at a time, as you will probably need to use them quite frequently when you are speaking French.

aller to go

je vais
tu vas
il/elle va
nous allons
vous allez
ils/elles vont

future: **j'irai**
perfect: **je suis allé(e)**

s'asseoir to sit down

je m'assieds
tu t'assieds
il/elle s'assied
nous nous asseyons
vous vous asseyez
ils/elles s'asseyent

future: **je m'assiérai**
perfect: **je me suis assis(e)**

avoir to have

j'ai
tu as
il/elle a
nous avons
vous avez
ils/elles ont

future: **j'aurai**
perfect: **j'ai eu**

*In questions, when two vowels come together, one at the end of the verb and the other at the beginning of the pronoun, you put hyphens and a "t" between them.

boire   to drink

je bois
tu bois
il/elle boit
nous buvons
vous buvez
ils/elles boivent

future: **je boirai**
perfect: **j'ai bu**

connaître   to know

je connais
tu connais
il/elle connaît
nous connaissons
vous connaissez.
ils/elles connaissent

future: **je connaîtrai**
perfect: **j'ai connu**

courir   to run

je cours
tu cours
il/elle court
nous courons
vous courez
ils/elles courent

future: **je courrai**
perfect: **j'ai couru**

croire   to believe

je crois
tu crois
il/elle croit
nous croyons
vous croyez
ils/elles croient

future: **je croirai**
perfect: **j'ai cru**

devoir   to have to

je dois
tu dois
il/elle doit
nous devons
vous devez
ils/elles doivent

future: **je devrai**
perfect: **j'ai dû**

dire   to say

je dis
tu dis
il/elle dit
nous disons
vous dîtes
ils/elles disent

future: **je dirai**
perfect: **j'ai dit**

écrire   to write

j'écris
tu écris
il/elle écrit
nous écrivons
vous écrivez
ils/elles écrivent

future: **j'écrirai**
perfect: **j'ai écrit**

être   to be

je suis
tu es
il/elle est
nous sommes
vous êtes
ils/elles sont

future; **je serai**
perfect: **j'ai été**

faire to do

je fais
tu fais
il/elle fait
nous faisons
vous faites
ils/elles font

future: **je ferai**
perfect: **j'ai fait**

lire to read

je lis
tu lis
il/elle lit
nous lisons
vous lisez
ils/elles lisent

future: **je lirai**
perfect: **j'ai lu**

mettre to put

je mets
tu mets
il/elle met
nous mettons
vous mettez
ils/elles mettent

future: **je mettrai**
perfect: **j'ai mis**

ouvrir to open

j'ouvre
tu ouvres
il/elle ouvre
nous ouvrons
vous ouvrez
ils/elles ouvrent

future: **j'ouvrirai**
perfect: **j'ai ouvert**

partir to leave

je pars
tu pars
il/elle part
nous partons
vous partez
ils/elles partent

future: **je partirai**
perfect: **je suis parti(e)**

pouvoir to be able to

je peux
tu peux
il/elle peut
nous pouvons
vous pouvez
ils/elles peuvent

future: **je pourrai**
perfect: **j'ai pu**

prendre to take

je prends
tu prends
il/elle prend
nous prenons
vous prenez
ils/elles prennent

future: **je prendrai**
perfect: **j'ai pris**

rire to laugh

je ris
tu ris
il/elle rit
nous rions
vous riez
ils/elles rient

future: **je rirai**
perfect: **j'ai ri**

savoir   to know

je sais
tu sais
il/elle sait
nous savons
vous savez
ils/elles savent

future: **je saurai**
perfect: **j'ai su**

sortir   to go out

je sors
tu sors
il/elle sort
nous sortons
vous sortez
ils/elles sortent

future: **je sortirai**
perfect: **je suis sorti(e)**

suivre   to follow

je suis
tu suis
il/elle suit
nous suivons
vous suivez
ils/elles suivent

future: **je suivrai**
perfect: **j'ai suivi**

venir   to come

je viens
tu viens
il/elle vient
nous venons
vous venez
ils/elles viennent

future: **je viendrai**
perfect: **je suis venu(e)**

vivre   to live

je vis
tu vis
il/elle vit
nous vivons
vous vivez
ils/elles vivent

future: **je vivrai**
perfect: **j'ai vécu**

voir   to see

je vois
tu vois
il/elle voit
nous voyons
vous voyez
ils/elles voient

future: **je verrai**
perfect: **j'ai vu**

vouloir   to want

je veux
tu veux
il/elle veut
nous voulons
vous voulez
ils/elles veulent

present: **je voudrai**
perfect: **j'ai voulu**

Phrase explainer

Throughout the illustrated section of this book, there are useful short phrases and everyday expressions. You may find these easier to remember if you understand the different words that make them up.

This section lists the expressions under the page number where they appeared (although those whose word for word meaning is like the English have been left out). After reminding you of the suggested English equivalent, it shows you how they break down and, wherever possible, gives you the literal translations of the words involved.* Any grammatical terms used (e.g. reflexive verb) are explained in the grammar section.

page 4
• **A tout à l'heure**   See you later:
à=until (and many other meanings); here **tout à l'heure**=in a moment (highly idiomatic).
• **faire la bise à**   to kiss:
faire=to make; **la bise**=kiss (colloquial for **le baiser**); à=to. Another way of saying "to kiss" is **embrasser**.

page 5
• **D'accord**   I agree/Agreed:
d' (**de** in front of consonants)=of; **l'accord** (m)=agreement.
• **Comment t'appelles-tu?**   What's your name?
comment?=how?; **s'appeler**=to call oneself (a reflexive verb).
• **Quel âge as-tu?**   How old are you?
quel(le)?=what?; **l'âge** (m)=age; **as-tu**=have you.
• **J'ai dix-neuf ans**   I'm nineteen:
j'ai=I have; **dix-neuf**=nineteen; **ans** (m)=years.

page 12
• **Je suis chez moi.**   I'm at home:
je suis=I am; **chez moi**=at me (to say "at home", use **chez** followed by **moi**=me, **toi/vous**=you, **lui/elle**=him/her, **nous**=us, **eux/elles**=them (m/f) according to whose home you are referring to).

page 18
• **ATTENTION, CHIEN MECHANT**   BEWARE OF THE DOG:
attention=attention, care (**faire attention**=to be careful); **le chien**=dog; **méchant**=bad, wicked.

page 26
• **A table!**   It's ready!
à=to; **la table**=table.
• **Servez-vous.**   Help yourselves:
se servir=to serve/help oneself.
• **Bon appétit!**   Enjoy your meal!
bon=good; **l'appétit** (m)=appetite. This is a polite phrase you say to people who are about to eat.
• **C'est très bon.**   It tastes good:
c'est=it's; **très**=very; **bon**=good.

page 37
• **Que désirez-vous?**   What would you like?
que?=what? (like **qu'est-ce que?**, but more polite); **désirez-vous**=want/wish you.
• **Service compris?**   Is service included?
le service=service; **compris**=included (full question: **Est-ce que le service est compris?**)
• **Service non compris**   Service not included:
non=no, not.

page 43
• **Ça fait...**   That will be...
ça=it, that (short for **cela**); **fait**=makes; this is another way of saying **ça coûte...** (see page 44).

*Literal meanings of French words are introduced by the sign =.

page 44
- **Vous désirez?** What would you like?
vous=you (polite); **désirez**=want/wish; (same meaning as **Que désirez-vous?** see page 37).
- **Je voudrais...** I would like...
vouloir=to want; this is how you ask for things in shops, restaurants, ticket offices etc..
- **C'est quelle taille?** What size is it?
c'est=it's; **quel(le)?**=what/which?; **la taille**=size.
- **Combien coûte...?** How much is...?
combien?=how much?; **coûte**=costs.
- **Ça coûte...** It costs...
ça=it, that (short for **cela**), e.g. **combien coûte cette robe?** How much is this dress?

page 48
- **Allô** Hello:
allô is only used on the telephone.
- **qui est à l'appareil?** who's speaking?
qui?=who?; **est**=is; **à**=at; **l'appareil (m)**=appliance, telephone (short for **l'appareil téléphonique**, now a little old fashioned).

page 49
- **Monsieur/Madame,** Dear Sir/Madam:
Monsieur=Sir, Mr; **Madame**=Madam/Mrs (note that you do not use **Cher/Chère**=dear (m/f) to open a formal letter).
- **Veuillez trouver ci-joint** Please find enclosed:
veuillez=would you/would you wish to (very polite, from **vouloir**); **trouver**=to find; **ci-joint**=enclosed.
- **Je vous prie de croire, Monsieur/Madame, à mes sentiments les meilleurs** Yours faithfully:
je vous prie=I beg you; **de croire à**=to believe in; **mes sentiments les meilleurs**=my best feelings/sentiments.
- **J'ai été très content(e) d'avoir de tes nouvelles.** It was lovely to hear from you:
j'ai été=I was; **très**=very;

content(e)=happy; **d'avoir**=to have; **de tes**=some of your; **les nouvelles**=news (**la nouvelle**=a piece of news).
- **Bons baisers,** Love from:
bon(ne)=good; **baiser**=kiss (Other common ways of ending an informal letter: **Je t'/vous embrasse**=I kiss you; **baisers affectueux**=affectionate kisses; **affectueusement**=affectionately).
- **Nous nous amusons beaucoup.** Having a lovely time:
nous nous amusons=we are having fun (**s'amuser**=to have fun/a good time); **beaucoup**=a lot.
- **Je pense bien à toi.** Thinking of you:
je pense à=I am thinking of; **bien**=well (in this expression, **bien** is used for emphasis, to mean "a lot" or "often"); **toi**=you.
- **appelle maison** phone home
appelle=phone/call; **maison**=house/home (see above, page 12; **à la maison** is another way of saying "at home").

page 50
- **Pour aller à?** Which way is...?
pour=for/(in order) to; **aller à**=to go to.
- **Est-ce que... est loin d'ici?** Is it far to...?
est-ce que=common way of opening a question (see page 102); **est-ce que...est?**=is?; **loin**=far; **d'ici**=from here (**ici**=here).

page 52
- **Stationnement interdit!** · No parking!
le stationnement=parking; **interdit(e)**=forbidden.

page 55
- **Non-fumeurs** No smoking:
=non-smokers.

page 78
- **Bon anniversaire** Happy birthday:
bon(ne)=good; **anniversaire**=birthday.

page 79
- **Joyeux Noël** Happy Christmas:
joyeux (joyeuse)=happy, joyful;
Noël=Christmas.
- **Merci beaucoup** Thank you very much:
merci=thank you; **beaucoup**: a lot/much.
- **Bonne année.** Happy New Year:
bon(ne)=good; **l'année (f)**=year. (Note that "year" can be either **l'année (f)** or **l'an (m)**, as in **le jour de l'An**).

page 82
- **Il commence à faire jour.** It is getting light:
il commence à=it is beginning to (note that **il** (he) can be used impersonally in this way, e.g. **il pleut**=it is raining); **faire jour**=to be light (**le jour** means "daylight" as well as "day", and **faire jour** is only used for natural light).
- **Il fait jour/nuit.** It is light/dark:
il fait=it is (literally=it makes, but **il fait** is commonly used to describe the weather; see examples on page 85); **jour**=day, daylight (see above); **nuit**=night, darkness.
- **La nuit tombe** It is getting dark:
la nuit=night; **tombe**=is falling.

page 83
- **Quelle heure est-il?** What time is it?
quel(le)?=what/which?; **heure**=hour; **est-il**=is it.
- **Il est une heure/trois heures.** It is one/three o'clock:
il est=it is; **un(e)**=one; **trois**=three; **heure(s)**=hour(s).
- **dix heures moins le quart** a quarter to ten:
dix heures=ten o'clock; **moins**=minus/less; **le quart**=quarter.
- **dix heures cinq/et quart/et demie** five/a quarter/half past ten:
dix heures=ten o'clock; **cinq**=five; **et quart**=and quarter; **et demie**=and half.

- **huit heures du matin/soir** 8 a.m./p.m.:
huit heures=eight o'clock; **du matin**=of the morning; **du soir**=of the evening.

page 84
- **Il pleut.** It's raining:
pleuvoir=to rain (see note on impersonal **il**, page 82).

page 85
- **Quel temps fait-il?** What is the weather like?
quel(le)?=what/which?; **temps**=weather (/time); **fait-il**=is it (see **Il fait jour,** page 82).
- **J'ai chaud.** I'm hot:
j'ai=I have; **chaud**=hot (**avoir**=to have is often used in such expressions, e.g. **j'ai froid/faim**=I am cold/hungry).
- **Il fait du vent/brouillard.** It's windy/foggy:
il fait=it makes/is (see **Il fait jour,** page 82) ; **du vent**=some wind; **du brouillard**=some fog.

English-French word list

Here you will find all the French words, phrases and expressions from the illustrated section of this book listed in English alphabetical order. Wherever useful, phrases and expressions are cross-referenced, and the words they are made up from are included in the list.

Following each French term, you will find its pronunciation in italics. To pronounce French properly, you need to listen to a French person speaking. This pronunciation guide will give you an idea as to how to pronounce new words and act as a reminder to words you have heard spoken.

When using the pronunciation hints in italics, read the "words" as if they were English, but bear in mind the following points:

- *a* is said like *a* in *cat*
- *ay* is like *a* in *date*
- *e(r)* is like *e* in *the* (not *thee*), and the *(r)* is not pronounced
- *ew* represents a sound unlike any English sound. It is a very sharp *u*. To make it, round your lips to say *oo*, then try to say *ee*
- *(n)* or *(m)* are used to show that the preceding vowel is nazalised: you make the sound through your nose and your mouth at the same time. The *n* or *m* are barely pronounced, rather like the *n* in *aunt*
- *g* in the pronunciation hints is always hard
- *k* represents a hard *c* as in *cat*
- remember that the French *r* is made by a roll in the back of your mouth; it sounds a little like gargling, but a bit harder. Any *r* in the pronunciation guide is said like this, except if it is in brackets: *(r)*
- *s* represents the hard *s* in *sea*
- *z* represents the *z* sound as in *zoo*
- *zh* represents the *j* sound in *treasure*.

A

to accelerate	accélérer	*ak-sel-ay-ray*
actor	l'acteur (m)	*lak-ter*
actress	l'actrice (f)	*lak-trees*
to add	additionner	*a-dee-see-on-ay*
address	l'adresse (f)	*la-dress*
advertisement (on poster)	l'affiche (f)	*la-feesh*
aeroplane	l'avion (m)	*lav-yo(n)*
Africa	l'Afrique (f)	*laf-reek*
afternoon, in the afternoon	l'après-midi (m or f)	*la-prey-mee-dee*
against	contre	*kontr*
age	l'âge (m)	*lazh*
I agree, agreed	d'accord	*da-kor*
air hostess	l'hôtesse (f) de l'air	*lo-tess de(r) lair*
air steward	le steward	*le(r) stew-war*
airline ticket	le billet d'avion	*le(r) bee-yay dav-yo(n)*
airmail	par avion	*par av-yo(n)*
airport	l'aéroport (m)	*la-ay-ropor*
aisle	l'allée (f)	*la-lay*
alarm clock	le réveil	*le(r) ray-vaye*
alone	seul(e)	*serl*
alphabet	l'alphabet (m)	*lal-fa-bay*
ambulance	l'ambulance (f)	*lam-bew-la(n)s*
among	parmi	*par-mee*
anchor	l'ancre (f)	*la(n)kr*
and	et	*ay*
animal	l'animal (m)	*lan-ee-mal*
ankle	la cheville	*la she(r)-vee-ye*
to answer	répondre	*ray-po(n)dr*
to answer the telephone	répondre au téléphone	*ray-po(n)dr-o-tay-lay-fon*
apple	la pomme	*la pom*
apple tree	le pommier	*le(r) pom-ee-ay*
apricot	l'abricot (m)	*la-bree-ko*
April	avril	*av-reel*
architect (m/f)	l'architecte (m)	*lar-shee-tekt*
area code	l'indicatif (m)	*la(n)-deek-at-eef*
arm	le bras	*le(r) bra*
armchair	le fauteuil	*le(r) fo-te(r)-ye*
Arrivals	Arrivées (f. pl)	*a-ree-vay*
art gallery	la galerie	*la gal-er-ee*
article (in newspaper)	l'article (m)	*lar-teekl*
to ask	demander	*de(r)-ma(n)-day*
to ask a question	poser une question	*pozay ewn kest-yo(n)*
to ask the way	demander le chemin	*de(r)-ma(n)-day le(r) she(r)-ma(n)*
to fall asleep	s'endormir	*sa(n)-dormeer*
at the seaside	au bord de la mer	*o bor de(r) la mair*
athletics	l'athlétisme (m)	*lat-lay-teesm*
Atlantic Ocean	l'Atlantique (m)	*lat-la(n)-teek*
attic	le grenier	*le(r) gren-ee-ay*
audience	les spectateurs (m)	*lay spekt-at-er*
August	août	*oot*
aunt	la tante	*la ta(n)t*
Australia	l'Australie (f)	*los-tral-ee*
autumn	l'automne (m)	*lo-tonn*
away from (e.g. to run away from)	de (e.g. s'échapper de)	*de(r) (say-shap-ay de(r))*

B

English	French	Pronunciation
baby	le bébé	le(r) bay-bay
back	le dos	le(r) do
to do back-stroke	nager sur le dos	nazhay sewr le(r) do
backwards	en arrière	an a-ree-air
bait	l'amorce (f)	la-morse
bakery	la boulangerie	la boo-la(n)-zher-ee
balcony	le balcon	le(r) bal-ko(n)
with balcony	avec balcon	avek bal-ko(n)
bald	chauve	shov
to be bald	être chauve	et-re(r) shov
ball	la balle	la bal
ballet	le ballet	le(r) balay
ballet dancer (m)	le danseur de ballet	le(r) da(n)-ser de(r) balay
ballet dancer (f)	la danseuse de ballet	la da(n)-serz de(r) balay
balloon	le ballon	le(r) bal-o(n)
banana	la banane	la ban-an
bandage	le bandage	le(r) ba(n)-dazh
bank (river)	la rive	la reev
bank	la banque	la ba(n)k
bank manager	le directeur de banque	le(r) deer-ek-ter de(r) ba(n)k
barefoot	pieds nus	pee-ay new
a bargain	une bonne affaire	ewn bona-fair
to bark	aboyer	a-bwa-yay
barn	la grange	la gra(n)zh
barrier	la barrière	la ba-ree-air
basement	le sous-sol	le(r) soo-sol
basket	le panier	le(r) pa-nee-ay
bath	le bain	le(r) ba(n)
to have a bath	prendre un bain	pra(n)-dro(n) ba(n)
to run a bath	faire couler un bain	fair koolay o(n) ba(n)
bathmat	la descente de bain	la day-sa(n)t de(r) ba(n)
bathrobe	le peignoir de bain	le payn-war de(r) ba(n)
bathroom	la salle de bain	la sal de(r) ba(n)
with bathroom	avec salle de bain	avek sal de(r) ba(n)
to be	être	et-re(r)
to be born	naître	nay-tr
to be called , to be named	s'appeler	sa-pel-ay
to be fit	être en forme	et-re(r) a(n) form
to be fond of	aimer bien	ay-may bee-a(n)
to be frozen	être gelé(e)	et-re(r) zhe(r)-lay
to be happy	être heureux (f: heureuse)	et-re(r) er-e(r) (er-erz)
to be hungry	avoir faim	av-war fa(m)
to be late	être en retard	et-re(r) a(n) re-tar
to be on time	arriver à l'heure	a-reev-ay a ler
to be seasick	avoir le mal de mer	av-war le(r) mal de(r) mair
to be sick	vomir	vo-meer
to be sleepy	avoir sommeil	av-war som-aye
to be thirsty	avoir soif	av-war swaf
beach	la plage	la plazh
beak	le bec	le(r) bek
beans	les haricots (m)	lay a-ree-ko
beard	la barbe	la barb
to have a beard	porter la barbe	por-tay la barb
beautiful	beau (belle)	bo (bell)
bed	le lit	le(r) lee
to go to bed	aller au lit	a-lay o lee
bedroom	la chambre	la sha(m) br
bedside lamp	la lampe de chevet	la la(m)p de(r) she(r)-vay
bedside table	la table de chevet	la tabl de(r) she(r)-vay
bedspread	le dessus-de-lit	le(r) de(r)-sew de(r) lee
bedtime	l'heure (f) d'aller se coucher	ler da-lay se(r) koo-shay
bee	l'abeille (f)	la-baye
beer	la bière	la bee-air
behind	derrière	dare-ee-air
Belgium	la Belgique	la belzh-eek
bell	la cloche	la klosh
doorbell	la sonnette	la son-et
to belong to	être membre de	et-re(r) ma(m)br de(r)
belt	la ceinture	la sa(n)-tewr
safety belt, seatbelt	la ceinture de sécurité	la sa(n)-tewr de(r) say-kewr-ee-tay
bench	le banc	le(r) ba(n)
beside	à côté de	a ko-tay de(r)
better	mieux	mee-e(r)
to feel better	se sentir mieux	se(r) sa(n)-teer mee-e(r)
between	entre	a(n)tr
Beware of the dog	Attention, chien méchant	A-te(n)see-o(n) shee-a(n) may-sha(n)
bicycle	la bicyclette	la bee-see-klet
big	grand(e)	gra(n)
bill	l'addition (f)	la-dee-see-o(n)
bin	la boîte à ordures	la bwat a or-dewr
biology	la biologie	la bee-ol-ozh-ee
bird	l'oiseau (m)	lwa-zo
birth	la naissance	la nay-sa(n)s
birthday	l'anniversaire (m)	la-nee-vers-air
birthday card	la carte d'anniversaire	la kart da-nee-vers-air
Happy birthday	Bon anniversaire	bon annee-vers-air
biscuit	le biscuit	le(r) bees-kwee
bitter	amer (f: amère)	am-air
black	noir(e)	nwar
blackbird	le merle	le(r) mairl
blackboard	le tableau noir	le(r) tab-lo nwar
block of flats	l'immeuble (m)	lee-me(r)bl
blond	blond(e)	blo(n)
blond hair	les cheveux blonds	lay she(r)-ve(r) blo(n)
blouse	le chemisier	le(r) she(r)-mee-zee-ay
blue	bleu(e)	ble(r)
to board (ship, plane)	embarquer	a(m)-bar-kay
board game	le jeu de société	le(r) zhe(r) de(r) so-cee-ay-tay
boarding house	la pension	la pa(n)-see-o(n)
boat	le bateau	le(r) ba-to
to travel by boat	aller en bateau	a-lay a(n) ba-to
body	le corps	le(r) kor
bonnet (of car)	le capot	le(r) ka-po
book	le livre	le(r) lee-vr
picture book	le livre illustré	le(r) lee-vr ee lew-stray
booked up, fully booked	complet	kom-play
bookshop	la librairie	la lee-bray-ree
bookshop and stationer's	la librairie-papeterie	la lee-bray-ree-pa-pay-ter-ee

boot (of car)	le coffre	le(r) cofr
boots	les bottes (f)	lay bot
wellington boots	les bottes (f) de caoutchouc	lay bot de(r) cow-tshoo
boring	ennuyeux (ennuyeuse)	on-wee-ye(r) (on-wee-ye(r)z)
to be born	naître	nay-tr
boss (m)	le patron	le(r) pa-tro(n)
boss (f)	la patronne	la pa-tron
bottle	la bouteille	la boo-taye
bouquet	le bouquet	le(r) boo-kay
boutique	la boutique	la boo-teek
bowl	le bol	le(r) bol
bowl (for goldfish)	le bocal	le(r) bok-al
box office	le guichet	le(r) gee-shay
boy	le garçon	le(r) gar-so(n)
bra	le soutien-gorge	le(r) soo-tee-a(n) gorzh
bracelet	le bracelet	le(r) bra-slay
branch	la branche	la bra(n)-sh
brave	courageux (courageuse)	koor-azhe(r) (koor-azh-e(r)z
bread	le pain	le(r) pa(n)
break (at school)	la récréation	la ray-kray-ass-ee-o(n)
to break	casser	kassay
to break your leg	se casser la jambe	se(r) kassay la zha(m)b
breakdown (vehicle)	la panne	la pan
to have a breakdown	tomber en panne	to(m)-bay a(n) pan
breakfast	le petit déjeuner	le(r) pe(r)-tee day-zhe(r)-nay
to do breast-stroke	nager la brasse	nazhay la brass
bride	la mariée	la mar-ee-ay
bridegroom	le marié	le(r) mar-ee-ay
bridge	le pont	le(r) po(n)
bright	vif (vive)	veef (veev)
to bring up	élever	ay-lev-ay
broad	large	larzh
brooch	la broche	la brosh
brother	le frère	le(r) frair
brown	brun(e)	bra(n) (brewn)
brown hair	les cheveux bruns	lay she(r)-ve(r) bra(n)
bruise	le bleu	le(r) ble(r)
brush (for painting)	le pinceau	le(r) pa(n)-so
brush	la brosse	la bross
toothbrush	la brosse à dents	la bross a da(n)
to brush your hair	se brosser les cheveux	se(r) brossay lay she(r)-ve(r)
Brussels sprout	le chou de Bruxelles	le(r) shoo de(r) brew-ksell
bucket	le seau	le(r) so
budgie	la perruche	la per-ewsh
buffet car	le wagon-restaurant	le(r) va-go(n) rest-or-a(n)
builder, worker (m)	l'ouvrier (m)	loo-vree-ay
builder, worker (f)	l'ouvrière (f)	loo-vree-air
building	le bâtiment	le(r) ba-tee-ma(n)
bulb (plant)	le bulbe	le(r) bewlb
bunch of flowers	le bouquet de fleurs	le(r) boo-kay de(r) fler
burn	la brûlure	la brew-lewr
to burst out laughing	éclater de rire	ay-klat-ay de(r) reer
bus	l'autobus (m)	lo-to-bews
bus stop	l'arrêt (m) d'autobus	la-ray do-to-bews
to take the bus	prendre l'autobus	pra(n)dr lo-to-bews

bush	le buisson	le(r) bwee-so(n)
busy	occupé(e)	o-kew-pay
bustling	affairé(e)	a-fair-ay
butcher's shop	la boucherie	la boosh-e(r)-ree
butter	le beurre	le(r) ber
buttercup	le bouton d'or	le(r) boo-to(n) dor
butterfly	le papillon	le(r) pa-pee-yo(n)
button	le bouton	le(r) boo-to(n)
to buy	acheter	ash-tay
by return of post	par retour du courrier	par retoor dew koor-ee-ay

C

cabbage	le chou (pl: les choux)	le(r) shoo (lay shoo)
cabin	la cabine	la ka-been
cage	la cage	la kazh
cake	le gâteau	le(r) ga-to
cake shop	la pâtisserie	la pa-tee-ser-ee
to calculate	faire des calculs	fair day kal-kewl
calculator	la machine à calculer	la masheen a kal-kewlay
calendar	le calendrier	le(r) ka-le(n)-dree-ay
calf	le veau	le(r) vo
camel	le chameau	le(r) sham-o
camera	l'appareil (m) photo	lapa-raye foto
to camp, to go camping	camper	ca(m)-pay
campsite	le camping	le(r) ca(m)-pee(n)g
Can I help you?	Vous désirez?	voo day-zeer-ay
Canada	le Canada	le(r) kan-a-da
candle	la bougie	la boo-zhee
canoe	le canoë	le(r) canoo-ay
cap	la casquette	la kas-kett
capital letter	la majuscule	la ma-zhews-kewl
to capsize	chavirer	sha-vee-ray
captain	le capitaine	le(r) ka-pee-ten
car	la voiture	la vwa-tewr
car-park	le parking	le(r) par-king
caravan	la caravane	la kar-avan
card	la carte	la kart
postcard	la carte postale	la kart post-al
credit card	la carte de crédit	la kart de(r) kray-dee
card (playing card)	la carte	la kart
to play cards	jouer aux cartes	zhoo-ay o kart
cardigan	le gilet	le(r) zhee-lay
careful	soigneux (soigneuse)	swan-ye(r) (swan-yerz)
careless	négligent(e)	nay-glee-zha(n)
caretaker (m/f)	le/la concierge	le(r)/la kon-see-yerzh
cargo	la cargaison	la kar-gay-so(n)
carpet	le tapis	le(r) ta-pee
fitted carpet	la moquette	la mo-ket
carriage	le wagon	le(r) va-go(n)
carrier-bag	le sac	le(r) sak
to carry	porter	por-tay
carrot	la carotte	la kar-ot
cashier (m)	le caissier	le(r) kay-see-ay
cashier (f)	la caissière	la kay-see-air
cassette	la cassette	la kass-et
cassette recorder	le magnétophone	le(r) man-yet-o-fon
casualty department	le service des urgences	le(r) ser-vees dez ewr-zha(n)s
cat	le chat	le(r) sha
to catch	attraper	a-trap-ay

English	French	Pronunciation
to catch a fish	attraper un poisson	a-trap-ay a(n) pwa-sso(n)
to catch the train	prendre le train	pra(n)-dr le(r) tra(n)
cathedral	la cathédrale	la ka-tay-dral
cauliflower	le chou-fleur	le(r) shoo-fler
to celebrate	célébrer	say-lay-bray
cellar	la cave	la kav
cello	le violoncelle	le(r) vee-ol-o(n)-sel
to play the cello	jouer du violoncelle	zhoo-ay dew vee-ol-o(n) sel
cemetery	le cimetière	le(r) seem-tee-air
centimetre	le centimètre	le(r) sa(n)-tee-metr
centre (politics)	le centre	le(r) sa(n)-tr
chair	la chaise	la shayz
chairlift	le télésiège	le(r) tay-lay-see-ezh
chalk	la craie	la kray
change (money)	la monnaie	la mon-ay
Have you any small change?	Avez-vous de la petite monnaie?	avay-voo de(r) la pe(r)-teet mon-ay
to change money	changer de l'argent	sha(n)-zhay de(r) lar-zha(n)
channel (TV and radio)	la chaîne	la shayn
to chase	courir après	koo-reer a-pray
to chat	bavarder	bav-ar-day
check-in	l'enregistrement (m)	la(n)-rezh-eest-re-ma(n)
checkout	la caisse	la kayss
cheek	la joue	la zhoo
cheerful	heureux (heureuse)	er-e(r) (er-erz)
cheese	le fromage	le(r) from-azh
chemist	la pharmacie	la far-ma-see
chemistry	la chimie	la shee-mee
cheque	le chèque	le(r) shek
to write a cheque	faire un chèque	fair a(n) shek
cheque-book	le carnet de chèques	le(r) kar-nay de(r) shek
cherry	la cerise	la ser-eez
to play chess	jouer aux échecs	zhoo-ay oz-ay-shek
chest	la poitrine	la pwa-treen
chicken	le poulet	le(r) poo-lay
child	l'enfant (m)	la(n)-fa(n)
childhood	l'enfance (f)	la(n)-fa(n)ce
chimney	la cheminée	la she(r)-mee-nay
chin	le menton	le(r) ma(n)-to(n)
China	la Chine	la sheen
chocolate	le chocolat	le(r) shok-o-la
choir	le choeur	le(r) ker
Christmas	Noël	no-wel
Christmas carol	le chant de Noël	le(r) sha(n) de(r) no-wel
Christmas Day	le jour de Noël	le(r) zhoor de(r) no-wel
Christmas Eve	la veille de Noël	la vey de(r) no-wel
Happy Christmas	Joyeux Noël	zhwa-ye(r) no-wel
Christmas tree	le sapin de Noël	le(r) sa-pa(n) de(r) no-wel
chrysanthemum	le chrysanthème	le(r) kree-sa(n)-tem
church	l'église (f)	lay-gleez
cinema	le cinéma	le(r) see-nay-ma
to go to the cinema	aller au cinéma	alay o see-nay-ma
circle	le cercle	le(r) serkl
city	la grande ville	la gra(n)d veel
to clap	applaudir	a-plod-eer
classroom	la salle de classe	la sal de(r) klass
claw	la griffe	la greef
clean	propre	propr
to clean your teeth	se brosser les dents	se(r) bross-ay lay da(n)
climate	le climat	le(r) klee-ma
to climb	grimper	gra(m)-pay
to climb (mountain climbing)	escalader	ays-kal-aday
to climb a tree	grimper un arbre	gra(m)-pay a-narbr
climber	l'alpiniste (m or f)	lal-peen-eest
cloakroom	le vestiaire	le(r) vest-ee-air
clock	la pendule	la pa(n)-dewl
alarm clock	le réveil	le(r) ray-vaye
to close	fermer	fair-may
clothes, clothing	les vêtements (m)	lay vayt-ma(n)
clothes peg	la pince à linge	la pa(n)ss a la(n)zh
cloud	le nuage	le(r) new-azh
coach	l'autocar (m)	lot-o-kar
coat	le manteau	le(r) ma(n)-to
cock	le coq	le(r) kok
coffee	le café	le(r) kaf-ay
coffee-pot	la cafetière	la kafe(r)-tee-air
coin	la pièce de monnaie	la pee-ayss de(r) mon-ay
cold	froid(e)	frwa
It's cold.	Il fait froid.	eel fay frwa
cold water	l'eau (f) froide	lo frwad
to have a cold	être enrhumé(e)	et-re(r) o(n)-rewm-ay
to collect	faire collection de	fair kol-ek-see-yo(n) de(r)
to collect stamps	faire collection de timbres	fair kol-ek-see-yon de(r) ta(m)br
collection	la collection	la kol-ek-see-yon
collection times (post)	les heures (f) de levée	layz er de(r) lev-ay
collision	la collision	la kol-ee-zee-yon
colour	la couleur	la koo-ler
comb	le peigne	le(r) payn-ye(r)
to comb your hair	se peigner les cheveux	se(r) payn-yay lay she(r)-ve(r)
comic (book)	le journal illustré	le(r) zhoor-nal ee-lewst-ray
complexion	le teint	le(r) ta(n)
computer	l'ordinateur (m)	lord-ee-nat-er
computer studies	l'informatique (f)	la(n)-form-at-eek
conductor (orchestra) (m/f)	le chef d'orchestre	le(r) shef dor-kestr
cone	le cône	le(r) kon
to congratulate	féliciter	fay-lees-ee-tay
continent	le continent	le(r) co(n)-tee-na(n)
to cook	faire la cuisine	fair la kwee-zeen
corner	le coin	le(r) kwa(n)
to cost	coûter	coo-tay
It costs...	Ça coûte...	sa coot
cot	le lit d'enfant	le(r) lee da(n)-fa(n)
cottage	la chaumière	la shom-ee-air
cotton	le coton	le(r) kot-o(n)
cotton, made of cotton	en coton	a(n) kot-o(n)
counter	le comptoir	le(r) ko(m)-twar
country	le pays	le(r) pay-ee
countryside	la campagne	la ka(m)-pan-ye
cousin (m)	le cousin	le(r) kooz-a(n)
cousin (f)	la cousine	la kooz-een
cow	la vache	la vash
cowshed	l'étable (f)	lay-tabl
crab	le crabe	le(r) krab
to crawl, to do the crawl	nager le crawl	nazh-ay le(r) krawl
crayon	le crayon de couleur	le(r) kray-o(n) de(r) koo-ler
cream	la crème	la krem

English	French	Pronunciation
credit card	la carte de crédit	la kart de(r) kray-dee
crew	l'équipage (m)	lay-keep-azh
cross, angry	fâché(e)	fa-shay
to cross the street	traverser la rue	tra-ver-say la rew
crossing (sea)	la traversée	la tra-ver-say
crowd	la foule	la fool
to cry	pleurer	pler-ay
cup	la tasse	la tass
cupboard	le placard	le(r) pla-kar
to cure	guérir	gay-reer
curly	frisé(e)	free-zay
curly hair	les cheveux (m) frisés	lay she(r)-ve(r) free-zay
curtain	le rideau	le(r) ree-do
customer (m)	le client	le(r) klee-a(n)
customer (f)	la cliente	la klee-aunt
customs	la douane	la doo-ann
customs officer (m/f)	le douanier	le(r) doo-an-ee-ay
cut (wound)	la blessure	la bless-ewr

D

English	French	Pronunciation
daffodil	la jonquille	la zho(n)-kee-ye(r)
daisy	la pâquerette	la pa-ker-ett
to dance	danser	da(n)-say
dance floor	la piste de danse	la peest de(r) da(n)s
dark (colour)	foncé(e)	fo(n)-say
dark (complexion)	brun(e)	bra(n) (brewn)
It is dark.	Il fait nuit.	eel fay nwee
It is getting dark.	La nuit tombe.	la nwee to(m)b
date	la date	la dat
daughter	la fille	la fee-ye(r)
only daughter	la fille unique	la fee-ye(r) ew-neek
dawn	l'aube (f)	lobe
day, daytime, in the daytime	le jour	le(r) zhoor
the day after tomorrow	après-demain	a-pray-de(r)ma(n)
the day before yesterday	avant-hier	a-va(n)-teeyair
Dear...	Cher... (Chère...)	shair
Dear Sir/Madam	Monsieur/Madame,	me(r)-syur/ma-dam
death	la mort	la mor
December	décembre	day-sa(m)br
deck	le pont	le(r) po(n)
deep	profond(e)	pro-fo(n)
delicatessen	la charcuterie	la shar-kew-ter-ee
delicious	délicieux (délicieuse)	day-lee-see-ye(r) (day-lee-see-erz)
to deliver	distribuer	dees-tree-bew-ay
democratic	démocratique	day-mo-krat-eek
dentist (m/f)	le/la dentiste	le(r)/la da(n)-teest
department (in shop)	le rayon	le(r) ray-o(n)
department store	le grand magasin	le(r) gra(n) mag-az-a(n)
Departures	Départs (m. pl)	day-par
desert	le désert	le(r) day-zer
designer (m)	le dessinateur	le(r) day-seen-at-er
designer (f)	la dessinatrice	lay day-seen-at-rees
dessert, pudding	le dessert	le(r) day-ser
to dial 999	appeler police secours	apel-ay pol-ees se(r)-koor

English	French	Pronunciation
diary	l'agenda (m)	lazh-a(n)-da
to die	mourir	moo-reer
different	différent(e)	dee-fer-e(n)
difficult	difficile	dee-fee-seel
to dig	creuser	kre(r)-zay
dining room	la salle à manger	la sal-a-ma(n)zhay
dirty	sale	sal
disc jockey	le disc jockey	le(r) disk-zhok-ee
discothèque	la boîte	la bwat
to go to a discothèque	aller dans une boîte	a-lay da(n)z ewn bwat
district	le quartier	le(r) kar-tee-ay
to dive	plonger	plo(n)-zhay
to divide	diviser	dee-vee-zay
divided by (maths)	divisé par	dee-vee-zay par
diving board	le plongeoir	le(r) plo(n)-zhwar
to do	faire	fair
to do back-stroke	nager sur le dos	na-zhay sewr le(r) do
to do breast-stroke	nager la brasse	na-zhay la brass
to do the gardening	faire le jardinage	fair le(r) zhar-deen-azh
to do odd jobs	bricoler	bree-kol-ay
docks, quay	le dock	le(r) dok
doctor (m/f)	le médecin	le(r) mayde(r)-sa(n)
dog	le chien	le(r) shee-a(n)
donkey	l'âne (m)	lan
door	la porte	la port
front door	la porte d'entrée	la port da(n)-tray
doorbell	la sonnette	la son-et
doormat	le paillasson	le(r) pa-yass-on(n)
double room	une chambre pour deux personnes	ewn sha(m)br poor de(r) per-son
doughnut	le beignet	le(r) ben-yay
down	en bas	a(n) ba
downstairs	en bas	a(n) ba
to go downstairs	descendre l'escalier	day-se(n)dr less-kal-ee-ay
dragonfly	la libellule	la lee-bell-ewl
to play draughts	jouer aux dames	zhoo-ay o dam
to dream	rêver	ray-vay
dress	la robe	la rob
to get dressed	s'habiller	sa-bee-yay
dressing gown	le peignoir	le(r) pay-nwar
to drink	boire	bwar
to drive	conduire	ko(n)-dweer
driver (m/f)	le chauffeur	le(r) sho-fer
to drop	laisser tomber	lay-say to(m)bay
drum	le tambour	le(r) ta(m)-boor
to play the drums	jouer du tambour	zhoo-ay dew ta(m)-boor
to dry, to wipe	essuyer	ay-swee-yay
to dry your hair	se sécher les cheveux	se(r) say-shay lay she(r)-ve(r)
to dry yourself	s'essuyer	ses-wee-yay
duck	le canard	le(r) kan-ar
dull	terne	tairn
dungarees	la salopette	la sal-o-pet
dustman	le boueux	le(r) boo-e(r)
duty-free shop	le magasin hors-taxe	le(r) mag-az-a(n) or-taks
duvet	la couette	la koo-et

E

English	French	Pronunciation
eagle	l'aigle (m)	lay-gle(r)
ear	l'oreille (f)	lor-aye
earrings	les boucles (f) d'oreille	lay bookl dor-aye

English	French	Pronunciation
east	l'est (m)	lest
Easter	Pâques	pak
easy	facile	fa-seel
to eat	manger	ma(n)-zhay
to have eaten well	avoir bien mangé	awar bee-a(n) ma(n)-zhay
egg	l'oeuf (m) (pl: les oeufs)	lu(r)f (lay-ze(r))
eight	huit	weet
8 in the morning, 8 a.m.	huit heures du matin	weet er dew ma-ta(n)
8 in the evening, 8 p.m.	huit heures du soir	weet er dew swar
eighteen	dix-huit	dee-zweet
eighty	quatre-vingts	katr-va(n)
elbow	le coude	le(r) kood
election	l'élection (f)	lay-lek-see-o(n)
electricity	l'électricité (f)	lel-ek-tree-see-tay
elephant	l'éléphant (m)	lel-ay-fa(n)
eleven	onze	o(n)z
emergency, catastrophe	la catastrophe	la cat-ass-trof
to employ someone	engager quelqu'un	a(n)-gazhay kel-ka(n)
employee (m)	l'employé (m)	lom-ploy-ay
employee (f)	l'employée (f)	lom-ploy-ay
empty	vide	veed
to empty	vider	veed-ay
Encore!	Bis!	bees
to get engaged	se fiancer	se(r) fee-a(n)-say
engine (train)	la locomotive	la lok-o-mot-eev
English (language or subject)	l'anglais (m)	la(n)-glay
to enjoy, to like	beaucoup aimer	bo-koo ay-may
Enjoy your meal!	Bon appétit!	bo(n) a-pay-tee
to enjoy yourself, to have fun	bien s'amuser	bee-a(n) sam-ewz-ay
enormous	énorme	ay-norm
entrance	l'entrée (f)	la(n)-tray
no entry (road sign)	sens interdit (f)	so(n)s a(n)-ter-dee
envelope	l'enveloppe (f)	la(n)-vel-op
Equator	l'Equateur (m)	lay-kwa-ter
escalator	l'escalier (m) roulant	lays-kal-ee-ay roo-la(n)
Europe	l'Europe (f)	ler-op
evening	le soir	le(r) swar
this evening	ce soir	se(r) swar
8 in the evening	huit heures du soir	weet er dew swar
exam	l'examen (m)	lex-am-a(n)
to fail an exam	rater un examen	ra-tay o(n) ez-am-a(n)
to pass an exam	être reçu(e) à un examen	et-re(r) re(r)-su a on ex-am-a(n)
to sit an exam	passer un examen	pa-say on ex-am-a(n)
exchange rate	le cours du change	le(r) koor dew sha(n)zh
to exercise	faire du keepfit	fair dew keep-fit
exercise book	le cahier	le(r) ka-yay
exhibition	l'exposition (f)	lex-poz-ee-see-o(n)
exit	la sortie	la sor-tee
expensive	cher (chère)	shair (shair)
It's expensive.	C'est cher.	say shair
eye	l'oeil (m) (pl: les yeux)	lu-ye (lay-zye(r))

F

English	French	Pronunciation
fabric	le tissu	le(r) tee-sew
face	la figure	la fee-gewr
factory	l'usine (f)	lew-zeen
to fail an exam	rater un examen	ra-tay o(n) ex-am-a(n)
to faint	s'évanouir	say-van-weer
fair, blond	blond(e)	blo(n) (blo(n)d)
to fall asleep	s'endormir	sa(n)-dor-meer
false	faux (fausse)	fo (fos)
family	la famille	la fa-mee-ye(r)
famous	célèbre	say-laybr
far	loin	lwa(n)
far away from	loin de	lwa(n) de(r)
Is it far to (...)?	Est-ce que (...) est loin d'ici?	ay-se-ke . . . ay lwa(n) dee-see
fare	le prix de la course	le(r) pree de(r) la koors
farm	la ferme	la fairm
farmer (m)	le fermier	le(r) fairm-ee-ay
farmer (f), farmer's wife	la fermière	la fairm-ee-air
farmhouse	la ferme	la fairm
farmyard	la basse-cour	la bass-koor
fashionable	à la mode	a la mod
fast	rapide	ra-peed
Fasten your seatbelts.	Attachez vos ceintures.	a-ta-shay vo sa(n)-tewr
fat	gros(se)	gro (gros)
father	le père	le(r) pair
feather	la plume	la plewm
February	février	fev-ree-ay
to feed	donner à manger (à)	don-ay a ma(n)-zhay (a)
to feel better	se sentir mieux	se se(n)-teer mee-ye(r)
to feel ill	se sentir malade	se se(n)-teer mal-ad
ferry	le carferry	le(r) kar fair-ee
to fetch	aller chercher	a-lay sher-shay
field	le champ	le(r) sha(m)
fifteen	quinze	ka(n)z
the fifth (for dates only)	le cinq	le(r) sa(n)k
fifty	cinquante	sa(n)k-o(n)t
to fill	remplir	ro(m)-pleer
to fill up with petrol	faire le plein	fair le(r) pla(n)
to have a filling	se faire plomber une dent	se(r) fair plo(m)-bay ewn da(n)
film (for camera)	la pellicule	la pel-ee-kewl
film (cinema)	le film	le(r) feelm
It's fine.	Il fait beau.	eel fay bo
finger	le doigt	le(r) dwa
fir tree	le sapin	le(r) sa-pa(n)
fire	le feu	le(r) fe(r)
fire (emergency)	l'incendie (m)	la(n)-sa(n)-dee
fire engine	la pompe à incendie	la po(m)p a a(n)-sa(n)-dee
to fire someone	renvoyer quelqu'un	ro(n)-vwa-yay kel-ka(n)
fire station	la caserne de pompiers	la kaz-ern de(r) po(m)-pee-ay
fireman	le pompier	le(r) po(m)-pee-ay
fireplace	la cheminée	la she(r)-mee-nay

English	French	Pronunciation
the first	le premier (f: la première)	le(r) prem-ee-ay (la prem-ee-air)
first class	première classe (f)	prem-ee-air klas
first floor	le premier étage	le(r) prem-ee-ay ay-tazh
first name	le prénom	le(r) pray-no(m)
fish	le poisson	le(r) pwa-so(n)
to go fishing	aller à la pêche	a-lay a la pesh
fishing boat	le bateau de pêche	le(r) ba-to de(r) pesh
fishing rod	la canne à pêche	la kan a pesh
fishmonger	la poissonnerie	la pwa-son-er-ee
to be fit	être en forme	et-re(r) a(n) form
fitted carpet	la moquette	la mok-et
five	cinq	sa(n)k
five past 10	dix heures cinq	dee-zer sa(n)k
flag	le drapeau	le(r) dra-po
flannel	le gant de toilette	le(r) ga(n) de(r) twa-let
flat	l'appartement (m)	la-par-te-ma(n)
block of flats	l'immeuble (m)	lee-merbl
flat tyre	le pneu crevé	le(r) pne(r) krev-ay
flavour, taste	le goût	le(r) goo
to float	flotter	flot-ay
flock	le troupeau	le(r) troo-po
flood	l'inondation (f)	leen-o(n)-da-see-o(n)
floor	le plancher	le(r) pla(n)-shay
ground floor	le rez-de-chaussée	le(r) ray de(r) sho-say
second floor	le deuxième étage	le(r) de(r)-zee-em ay-tazh
florist (m/f)	le/la fleuriste	le(r)/la fler-eest
flour	la farine	la far-een
flower	la fleur	la fler
bunch of flowers	le bouquet de fleurs	le boo-kay de(r) fler
flowerbed	le parterre	le(r) par-ter
flowered (with flower pattern)	à fleurs	a fler
fly	la mouche	la moosh
to fly	voler	vol-ay
fog	le brouillard	le(r) broo-yar
It's foggy.	Il fait du brouillard.	eel fay dew broo-yar
to follow	suivre	sweevr
to be fond of	aimer bien	ay-may bee-a(n)
foot	le pied	le(r) pee-ay
football (ball)	le ballon (de foot)	le(r) ba-lo(n) (de(r) foot)
to play football	jouer au football	zhoo-ay o foot -bal
forget-me-not	le myosotis	le(r) mee-o-zo-tees
fork (for eating)	la fourchette	la foor-shet
fork (for gardening)	la fourche	la foorsh
form	la fiche	la feesh
forty	quarante	kara(n)t
forwards	en avant	o(n) ava(n)
foundation cream	le fond de teint	le(r) fo(n) de(r) ta(n)
four	quatre	katr
the fourth (for dates only)	le quatre	le(r) katr
fourteen	quatorze	kat-orz
fox	le renard	le(r) ren-ar
fraction	la fraction	la frak-see-o(n)
France	la France	la fra(n)s
freckles	les taches (f) de rousseur	lay tash de(r) roo-sir
French (language or subject)	le français	le(r) fra(n)-say
French stick or bread	la baguette	la bag-et
fresh	frais (fraîche)	fray (fraysh)
Friday	vendredi (m)	vo(n)dr-dee
fridge	le frigidaire	le(r) freezh-ee-dair
friend (m)	l'ami (m)	la-mee
friend (f)	l'amie (f)	la-mee
friendly	sympathique	sa(m)-pa-teek
frightened	effrayé(e)	ay-fray-yay
fringe	la frange	la fra(n)zh
frog	la grenouille	la grenoo-ye(r)
front door	la porte d'entrée	la port da(n)-tray
frost	le gel	le(r) zhel
to frown	froncer les sourcils	fro(n)-say lay soor-see
frozen food	les produits (m) congelés	lay prod-wee co(n)-zhel-ay
to be frozen	être gelé(e)	et-re(r) zhelay
fruit	le fruit	le(r) frwee
fruit juice	le jus de fruit	le(r) zhew de(r) frwee
full	plein(e)	pla(n)
full stop	le point	le(r) pwa(n)
fully booked	complet	kom-play
to have fun	bien s'amuser	bee-a(n) sam-ew-zay
funeral	l'enterrement (m)	la(n)-ter-ma(n)
funnel (ship)	la cheminée	la she(r)-mee-nay
funny	drôle	drol
fur	la fourrure	la foor-ewr
furniture (furniture department)	ameublement (m)	amerb-le(r)-ma(n)
future	l'avenir (m)	laven-eer
in the future	à l'avenir	a laven-eer

G

English	French	Pronunciation
galaxy	la galaxie	la gal-ax-ee
art gallery	la galerie	la gal-e(r)-ree
game	le jeu (pl: les jeux)	le(r) zhe(r) (lay zhe(r))
gangway	la passerelle	la pas-e(r)-rel
garage	le garage	le(r) gar-azh
garden	le jardin	le(r) zhar-da(n)
garden shed	l'appentis (m)	la-pa(n)-tee
gardener (m)	le jardinier	le(r) zhar-deen-yay
to do the gardening	faire le jardinage	fair le(r) zhar-deen-azh
garlic	l'ail (m)	lie
gas	le gaz	le(r) gaz
gate	la barrière	la bar-ee-air
to gather speed	accélérer	ak-sel-air-ay
geography	la géographie	la zhay-og-ra-fee
geranium	le géranium	le(r) zhay-ran-ee-um
German (language or subject)	l'allemand (m)	lal-e(r)-ma(n)
Germany	l'Allemagne (f)	lal-e(r)-man-ye(r)
to get dressed	s'habiller	sa-bee-yay
to get engaged	se fiancer	se(r) fee-a(n)-say
to get married	se marier	se(r) mar-ee-ay
to get off (a bus or train)	descendre de	day-san(n)dr de(r)
to get on	monter dans	mo(n)-tay da(n)
to get undressed	se déshabiller	se(r) day-za-bee-yay

English	French	Pronunciation
to get up	se lever	se(r) le(r)-vay
giraffe	la girafe	la zheer-af
girl	la fille	la fee-ye(r)
to give	donner	don-ay
to give (a present)	offrir	off-reer
glass	le verre	le(r) vair
glasses, spectacles	les lunettes (f)	lay lewn-et
sunglasses	les lunettes (f) de soleil	lay lewn-et de(r) sol-ay
to wear glasses	porter des lunettes	por-tay day lewn-et
gloves	les gants (m)	lay ga(n)
to go	aller	a-lay
to go to bed	aller au lit	a-lay o lee
to go to the cinema	aller au cinéma	a-lay o sin-ay-ma
to go downstairs	descendre l'escalier	day-sa(n)dr less-kal-ee-yay
to go fishing	aller à la pêche	a-lay a la pesh
to go on holiday	aller en vacances	a-lay a(n) vak-a(n)ce
to go mountaineering	faire de l'alpinisme	fair de(r) lal-peen-eesm
to go upstairs	monter l'escalier	mon-tay less-kal-ee-yay
to go for a walk	faire une promenade	fair ewn pro-men-ad
to go window-shopping	faire du lèche-vitrines	fair dew lesh-veet-reen
to go to work	aller travailler	a-lay tra-vie-yay
goal	le but	le(r) bewt
goalkeeper	le gardien de but	le(r) gar-dee-a(n) de(r) bewt
goat	la chèvre	la shayvr
gold	l'or (m)	lor
made of gold	en or	o(n) or
goldfish	le poisson rouge	le(r) pwa-so(n) roozh
golf club	le club de golf	le(r) klub de(r) golf
to play golf	faire du golf	fair dew golf
good	bon(ne)	bo(n) (bon)
Good luck!	Bonne chance.	bo(n) sha(n)ce
Good-morning	Bonjour	bo(n)-zhoor
good value	bon marché	bo(n) mar-shay
It's good value.	C'est bon marché.	say bo(n) mar-shay
It tastes good.	C'est très bon.	say tray bo(n)
Goodbye	Au revoir	o re(r)-vwar
Good-night	Bonne nuit	bon nwee
goods train	le train de marchandises	le(r) tra(n) de(r) mar-sha(n)-deez
goose	l'oie (f)	lwa
gorilla	le gorille	le(r) gor-ee-ye(r)
government	le gouvernement	le(r) goov-ern-e(r)-ma(n)
grammar	la grammaire	la gram-air
granddaughter	la petite-fille	la pe(r)-teet fee-ye(r)
grandfather	le grand-père	le(r) gra(n)-pair
grandmother	la grand-mère	la gra(n)-mair
grandson	le petit-fils	le(r) pe(r)-tee-fees
grape	le raisin	le(r) ray-za(n)
grass	l'herbe (f)	lairb
Great Britain	la Grande-Bretagne	la gran(n)d-bret-an-ye(r)
green	vert(e)	vair
greenhouse	la serre	la sair
grey	gris(e)	gree
grocery shop	l'épicerie	lay-pees-e(r)-ree
ground floor	le rez-de-chaussée	le(r) ray de(r) sho-say
to growl	gronder	gro(n)-day
guard	le chef de train	le(r) shef de(r) tra(n)

English	French	Pronunciation
guest (m)	l'invité (m)	la(n)-veet-ay
guest (f)	l'invitée (f)	la(n)-veet-ay
guest house, boarding house	la pension	la pa(n)-see-o(n)
guinea pig	le cochon d'Inde	le(r) kosh-o(n) da(n)d
guitar	la guitare	la gee-tar
to play the guitar	jouer de la guitare	zhoo-ay de(r) la geetar
gymnastics	la gymnastique	la zheem-nast-eek

H

English	French	Pronunciation
hail	la grêle	la grel
to hail a taxi	appeler un taxi	a-pel-ay a(n) taks-ee
hair	les cheveux (m)	lay she(r)-ve(r)
to have (...) colour hair	avoir les cheveux (...)	avwar lay she(r)-ve(r)
hairdresser (m), hairdresser's	le coiffeur	le(r) kwaf-er
hairdresser (f), hairdresser's	la coiffeuse	la kwaf-erz
hairdrier	le séchoir à cheveux	le(r) say-shwar a she(r)-ve(r)
a half	un demi	a(n) de(r)-mee
half a kilo	une livre	ewn leevr
half a litre	un demi-litre	a(n) de(r)-mee-leetr
half past 10	dix heures et demie	deez er ay de(r)-mee
ham	le jambon	le(r) zha(m)-bo(n)
hammer	le marteau	le(r) mar-to
hamster	le hamster	le(r) am-stair
hand	la main	la ma(n)
handbag	le sac à main	le(r) sak a ma(n)
hand luggage	les baggages à main	lay bagazh a ma(n)
handsome	beau (belle)	bo (bell)
to hang on to	s'accrocher	sak-rosh-ay
to hang up (telephone)	raccrocher	ra-krosh-ay
happy	heureux (heureuse)	er-e(r) (er-erz)
to be happy	être heureux (heureuse)	et-re(r) er-e(r) (er-erz)
Happy birthday	Bon anniversaire	bo(n) a-nee-vair-sair
Happy New Year	Bonne année	bon a-nay
hard	dur(e)	dewr
hard-working	travailleur (travailleuse)	trav-ay-yer (trav-ay-yerz)
to harvest	faire la moisson	fair la mwa-so(n)
hat	le chapeau	le(r) sha-po
Have you any small change?	Avez-vous de la petite monnaie?	a-vay voo de(r) la pe(r)teet mo-nay
to have	avoir	avwar
to have a bath	prendre un bain	pra(n)dr a(n) ba(n)
to have a breakdown	tomber en panne	tom-bay a(n) pan
to have a cold	être enrhumé (e)	et-re(r) o(n)-rew-may
to have (...) colour hair	avoir les cheveux (...)	avwar lay she(r)-ve(r)
to have a filling	se faire plomber une dent	se(r) fair plo(m)-bay ewn da(n)
to have a flat tyre	avoir un pneu crevé	avwar a(n) pne(r) kre(r)-vay
to have fun	bien s'amuser	bee-a(n) sam-ew-zay
to have a shower	prendre une douche	pra(n)dr ewn doosh
to have stomach ache	avoir mal au ventre	avwar mal o va(n)tr
to have a temperature	avoir de la fièvre	avwar de(r) la fee-ayvr

116

English	French	Pronunciation
to have toothache	**avoir mal aux dents**	*avwar mal o da(n)*
Having a lovely time.	**Nous nous amusons beaucoup.**	*noo nooz am-ew-zo(n) bo-koo*
hay	**le foin**	*le(r) fwa(n)*
haystack	**la meule de foin**	*la me(r)l de(r) fwa(n)*
head	**la tête**	*la tet*
to have a headache	**avoir mal à la tête**	*avwar mal a la tet*
headband	**le bandeau**	*le(r) ba(n)-do*
headlight	**le phare**	*le(r) far*
headline	**le gros titre**	*le(r) gro teetr*
headmaster	**le directeur**	*le(r) dee-rek-ter*
headmistress	**la directrice**	*la dee-rek-trees*
headphones	**les écouteurs (m)**	*layz-ay-koo-ter*
healthy	**en bonne santé**	*o(n) bon sa(n)-tay*
heavy	**lourd(e)**	*loor (loord)*
to be heavy	**peser lourd**	*pe(r)-zay loor*
hedgehog	**le hérisson**	*le(r) ay-ree-so(n)*
heel	**le talon**	*le(r) ta-lo(n)*
height	**la hauteur**	*la ot-er*
Hello	**Bonjour**	*bo(n)-zhoor*
Hello (on phone)	**Allô**	*a-lo*
to help	**aider**	*aid-ay*
Help yourselves!	**Servez-vous.**	*sair-vay voo*
Can I help you?	**Vous désirez?**	*voo day-zee-ray*
hen	**la poule**	*la pool*
henhouse	**le poulailler**	*le(r) pool-aye-yay*
herbs	**les herbes (f) aromatiques**	*layz-erb arom-at-eek*
hero	**le héros**	*le(r) ay-ro*
heroine	**l'héroïne (f)**	*lair-o-een*
to hide	**se cacher**	*se(r) kash-ay*
hill	**la colline**	*la kol-een*
hippopotamus	**l'hippopotame (m)**	*leep-o-pot-am*
His name is...	**Il s'appelle...**	*eel sa-pel*
history	**l'histoire (f)**	*lees-twar*
hold (ship's)	**la cale**	*la kal*
to hold	**tenir**	*te(n)-eer*
holiday	**les vacances (f)**	*lay vak-a(n)s*
to go on holiday	**aller en vacances**	*a-lay o(n) vak-a(n)s*
honey	**le miel**	*le(r) mee-el*
honeymoon	**le voyage de noces**	*le(r) voy-azh de(r) noss*
hook (for fishing)	**le hameçon**	*le(r) am-so(n)*
horn	**le klaxon**	*le(r) klak-so(n)*
horse	**le cheval**	*le(r) she(r)-val*
horse racing	**les courses (f) hippiques**	*lay koors eep-eek*
hospital	**l'hôpital (m)**	*lop-ee-tal*
hot	**chaud(e)**	*sho*
hot water	**l'eau (f) chaude**	*lo shode*
I'm hot.	**J'ai chaud.**	*zhay sho*
hotel	**l'hôtel (m)**	*lo-tel*
to stay in a hotel	**rester à l'hôtel**	*ray-stay a lo-tel*
hour	**l'heure (f)**	*ler*
house	**la maison**	*la may-zo(n)*
How are you?	**Comment allez-vous?**	*kom-a(n)-tal-ay-voo*
how much...?	**combien...?**	*kom-bee-a(n)*
How much do I owe you?	**Combien je vous dois?**	*kom-bee-a(n) zhe(r) voo dwa*
How much is...?	**Combien coûte...?**	*kom-bee-a(n) koot*
How old are you?	**Quel âge as-tu?**	*kel azh a tew*
hump	**la bosse**	*la boss*
a hundred	**cent**	*sa(n)*
to be hungry	**avoir faim**	*avwar fa(m)*
to hurry	**se dépêcher**	*se(r) day-pesh-ay*
husband	**le mari**	*le(r) mar-ee*

I

English	French	Pronunciation
I agree	**D'accord.**	*dak-or*
I am sending (...) separately.	**Je t'envoie (...) séparément.**	*zhe(r) to(n)-vwa say-par-ay-mo(n)*
I'll call you back.	**Je te rappellerai.**	*zhe(r) te(r) ra-pel-er-ay*
I would like...	**Je voudrais...**	*zhe(r) voo-dray*
I'm nineteen.	**J'ai dix-neuf ans.**	*zhay deez-ne(r)f a(n)*
ice-cream	**la glace**	*la glass*
icicle	**le glaçon**	*le(r) glass-o(n)*
ill	**malade**	*ma-lad*
to feel ill	**se sentir malade**	*se(r) sa(n)-teer ma-lad*
important	**important(e)**	*am-port-a(n)*
in (for sports)	**in**	*een*
in	**dans**	*da(n)*
in focus	**au point**	*o pwa(n)*
in front of	**devant**	*de(r)-va(n)*
in the future	**à l'avenir**	*a laven-eer*
India	**l'Inde (f)**	*la(n)d*
indicator	**le clignotant**	*le(r) klee-nyo-ta(n)*
ingredient	**les ingrédients (m)**	*layz a(n)-gray-dee-o(n)*
injection	**la piqûre**	*la peek-ewr*
instrument	**l'instrument (m)**	*la(n)-strew-ma(n)*
inter-city train	**le rapide**	*le(r) ra-peed*
interesting	**intéressant(e)**	*a(n)-tay-ress-a(n)*
to interview	**interviewer**	*a(n)-ter-view-vay*
into	**dans**	*da(n)*
to introduce	**présenter**	*pray-sa(n)-tay*
to invite	**inviter**	*a(n)-vee-tay*
to iron	**repasser**	*re(r)-pass-ay*
Is it far to (...)?	**Est-ce que (...) est loin d'ici?**	*ay-se(r)-ke(r) lwa(n) dee-see*
Is service included?	**Service compris?**	*sair-vees kom-pree*
It costs...	**Ça coûte...**	*sa koot*
It is getting light.	**Il commence à faire jour.**	*eel kom-a(n)ce a fair zhoor*
It is light.	**Il fait jour.**	*eel fay zhoor*
It is 1 o'clock.	**Il est une heure.**	*eel ayt ewn er*
It is 3 o'clock.	**Il est trois heures.**	*eel ay trwaz-er*
It's...	**C'est...**	*say*
It's cold.	**Il fait froid.**	*eel fay frwa*
It's expensive.	**C'est cher.**	*say shair*
It's fine.	**Il fait beau.**	*eel fay bo*
It's foggy.	**Il fait du brouillard.**	*eel fay dew broo-yar*
It's good value.	**C'est bon marché.**	*say bo(n) marsh-ay*
It's raining.	**Il pleut.**	*eel ple(r)*
It's ready. (for meal)	**A table!**	*a tabl*
It's snowing.	**Il neige.**	*eel nayzh*
It's windy.	**Il fait du vent.**	*eel fay dew va(n)*
It was lovely to hear from you.	**J'ai été très content(e) d'avoir de tes nouvelles.**	*zhay ay-tay tray co(n)-ta(n) da-vwar de(r) tay noo-vel*
Italy	**l'Italie (f)**	*lee-tal-ee*

J

English	French	Pronunciation
jacket	**le blouson**	*le(r) bloo-zo(n)*
jam	**la confiture**	*la kon-fee-tewr*
January	**janvier**	*zha(n)-vee-yay*

Japan	le Japon	le(r) zha-po(n)
jeans	le jean	le(r) zheen
jewellery	les bijoux (m)	lay bee-zhoo
job, profession	le métier	le(r) may-tee-ay
to jog	faire du jogging	fair dew jogging
to join	s'inscrire à	sa(n)s-kreer a
journalist (m/f)	le/la journaliste	le(r)/la zhoor-nal-eest
judge (m/f)	le juge	le(r) zhewzh
juice	le jus	le(r) zhew
fruit juice	le jus de fruit	le(r) zhew de(r) frwee
jug	le pot	le(r) po
July	juillet	zhwee-yay
jumper	le pullover(-)	le(r) pewl-over
June	juin	zhwa(n)
jungle	la jungle	la zhu(n)gl

K

kangaroo	le kangourou	le(r) kang-oo-roo
to keep an eye on	surveiller	sewr-vay-yay
kennel	la niche	la neesh
keyboard	le clavier	le(r) klav-ee-yay
kilo	un kilo	o(n) kee-lo
A kilo of...	Un kilo de...	o(n) kee-lo de(r)
Half a kilo of...	Une livre de...	ewn leevr de(r)
to kiss	faire la bise à	fair la beez a
kitchen	la cuisine	la kwee-zeen
kitten	le chaton	le(r) sha-to(n)
knee	le genou	le(r) zhen-oo
to kneel down	s'agenouiller	sa-zhen-oo-yay
to be kneeling	être à genoux	et-re(r) a zhen-oo
knickers	le slip	le(r) sleep
knife	le couteau	le(r) koo-to
to knit	tricoter	tree-kot-ay
knitting needles	les aiguilles (f) à tricoter	layz ay-gwee-ye a tree-kot-ay
to knock over	renverser	ra(n)-vers-ay

L

label	l'étiquette (f)	let-ee-ket
labourer, worker	l'ouvrier (m)	loo-vree-yay
ladder	l'échelle (f)	lay-shel
lake	le lac	le(r) lak
lamb	l'agneau (m)	la(n)-yo
lamp	la lampe	la la(m)p
bedside lamp	la lampe de chevet	la la(m)p de(r) she(r)-vay
to land	atterrir	a-ter-eer
landlady	la propriétaire	la prop-ree-ay-tair
landlord	le propriétaire	le(r) prop-ree-ay-tair
landscape	le paysage	le(r) pay-zazh
large (clothes size)	grand	gra(n)
last	dernier (dernière)	der-nee-ay (der-nee-air)
late	en retard	o(n) re(r)-tar
to be late	être en retard	et-re(r) o(n) re(r)-tar
to laugh	rire	reer
to burst out laughing	éclater de rire	ay-klat-ay de(r) reer
lawn	la pelouse	la pel-ooz
lawnmower	la tondeuse	la to(n)-derz

lawyer (m/f)	l'avocat (m)	la-vo-ka
to lay eggs	pondre des oeufs	po(n)dr dayz e(r)
to lay the table	mettre le couvert	metr le(r) koo-vair
lazy	paresseux (paresseuse)	par-ayss-e(r) (par-ayss-erz)
leader (m/f)	le chef	le(r) shef
leaf	la feuille	la fe(r)-ye(r)
to lean on	s'appuyer sur	sa-pwee-yay sewr
to learn	apprendre	a-pre(n)dr
left luggage office	la consigne	la ko(n)-seen-ye(r)
on the left	à gauche	a goshe
left, left side	le côté gauche	le(r) ko-tay goshe
left wing, the left	la gauche	la goshe
leg	la jambe	la zha(m)b
leg of lamb	le gigot d'agneau	le(r) gee-go da(n)-yo
lemon	le citron	le(r) see-tro(n)
length	la longueur	la lo(n)-ger
lesson	le cours	le(r) koor
letter	la lettre	la letr
letter of alphabet	la lettre	la letr
letter box	la boîte aux lettres	la bwat o letr
library	la bibliothèque	la beeb-lee-o-tek
to lie down	s'allonger	sa-lonzh-ay
life	la vie	la vee
lifeguard	le maître nageur	le(r) may-tr nazh-er
lift	l'ascenseur (m)	la-sa(n)-sir
light (weight)	léger (légère)	lay-zhay (lay-zhair)
to be light (weight)	peser peu	pe(r)-zay pe(r)
light	la lumière	la lewm-ee-air
It is light.	Il fait jour.	eel fay zhoor
It is getting light.	Il commence à faire jour.	eel kom-a(n)s a fair zhoor
lightning	la foudre	la foodr
liner	le paquebot	le(r) pa-ke(r)-bo
lion	le lion	le(r) lee-o(n)
lip	la lèvre	la layvr
lipstick	le rouge à lèvres	le(r) roozh a layvr
list	la liste	la leest
to make a list	faire une liste	fair ewn leest
to listen	écouter	ay-koo-tay
to listen to music	écouter la musique	ay-koo-tay la mew-seek
to listen to the radio	écouter la radio	ay-koo-tay la ra-dee-o
litre	le litre	le(r) leetr
half a litre	un demi-litre	a(n) de(r)-mee-leetr
litter bin	la boîte à ordures	la bwat a or-dewr
to live	habiter	a-bee-tay
to live in a house	habiter une maison	a-bee-tay ewn may-zo(n)
lively	plein(e) d'entrain	pla(n) da(n)-tra(n)
living room	le salon	le(r) sa-lo(n)
to load	charger	shar-zhay
long	long (longue)	lo(n) (lo(n)-g)
to look at	regarder	re(r)-gar-day
to look for	chercher	sher-shay
loose (not tight)	large	larzh
lorry	le camion	le(r) kam-ee-o(n)
lorry driver (m/f)	le routier	le(r) roo-tee-ay
to lose	perdre	perdr
loudspeaker	le haut-parleur	le(r) o-par-ler
Love from... (end of letter)	Bons baisers,	bo(n) bay-zay
to love	aimer	ay-may
lovely, beautiful	beau (belle)	bo (bel)
luck	la chance	la sha(n)ce
Good luck	Bonne chance	bon sha(n)ce
luggage-rack	le filet	le(r) fee-lay

lullaby	la berceuse	la bear-serz
lunch	le déjeuner	le(r) day-zhe(r)-nay
lunch hour	l'heure (f) du déjeuner	ler dew day-zhe(n)-nay
to be lying down	être allongé(e)	et-re(r) a-lo(n)zh-ay

M

made of metal	en métal	a(n) may-tal
made of plastic	en plastique	a(n) plas-teek
magazine	le magazine	le(r) mag-a-zeen
mail	le courrier	le(r) koor-ee-ay
airmail	par avion	par av-ee-o(n)
main course	le plat principal	le(r) pla pra(n)-see-pal
main road, road	la route	la root
to make	faire	fair
to make a list	faire une liste	fair ewn leest
to make a telephone call, to dial	composer le numéro	kom-poz-ay le(r) new-may-ro
to make, to manufacture	fabriquer	fab-reek-ay
to put on make-up	se maquiller	se(r) ma-keyay
man	l'homme (m)	lom
map	la carte	la kart
March	mars	mars
margarine	la margarine	la mar-gar-een
market	le marché	le(r) mar-shay
market place	la place du marché	la plas dew mar-shay
to shop at the market	faire le marché	fair le(r) mar-shay
market stall	l'étalage	lay-tal-azh
marriage	le mariage	le(r) mar-ee-azh
to get married	se marier	se(r) mar-ee-ay
mascara	le mascara	le(r) mas-kar-a
maths	les maths (f)	lay mat
May	mai	may
meadow	la prairie	la pray-ree
measure	mesurer	me(r)-zew-ray
meat	la viande	la vee-a(n)d
mechanic (m)	le mécanicien	le(r) may-kan-ees-ee-a(n)
mechanic (f)	la mécanicienne	la may-kan-ees-ee-ayn
the media	les medias (m)	lay may-dee-a
medium (clothes size)	moyen	mo-ya(n)
to meet	rencontrer	ra(n)-ko(n)-tray
melon	le melon	le(r) me(r)-lo(n)
member (m/f)	le membre	le(r) ma(n)br
member of parliament (m/f)	le député	le(r) day-pew-tay
to mend	réparer	ray-par-ay
to mend (clothing)	racommoder	ray-kom-od-ay
menu	la carte	la kart
metal	le métal	le(r) may-tal
made of metal	en métal	o(n) may-tal
metre	le mètre	le(r) may-tr
to mew	miauler	mee-o-lay
midday	midi	mee-dee
midnight	minuit	mee-nwee
milk	le lait	le(r) lay
to milk the cows	traire les vaches	trair lay vash
a million	un million	a(n) mee-lee-yo(n)
mineral water	l'eau (f) minérale	Jo mee-nay-ral

minus (maths)	moins	mwa(n)
minute	la minute	la mee-newt
mirror	la glace	la glas
miserable	malheureux (malheureuse)	mal-er-e(r) (mal-er-erz)
to miss the train	manquer le train	ma(n)-kay le(r) tra(n)
to mix	mélanger	may-la(n)-zhay
model (m/f)	le mannequin	le(r) man-e(r)-ka(n)
mole	la taupe	la toep
Monday	lundi (m)	lo(n)-dee
money	l'argent (m)	lar-zha(n)
to change money	changer de l'argent	sha(n)-zhay de(r) lar-zha(n)
to put money in the bank	mettre de l'argent en banque	metr de(r) lar-zhan a(n) ba(n)k
to take money out	retirer de l'argent	re(r)-tee-ray de(r) lar-zhan(n)
monkey	le singe	le(r) sa(n)zh
month	le mois	le(r) mwa
moon	la lune	la lewn
moped	la mobylette	la mo-bee-let
morning, in the morning	le matin	le(r) ma-ta(n)
8 in the morning, 8 a.m.	huit heures du matin	weet er dew ma-ta(n)
this morning	ce matin	se(r) ma-tan
mosquito	le moustique	le(r) moos-teek
mother	la mère	la mair
motor racing	les courses (f) d'auto	lay koors do-to
motorbike	la moto	la mo-to
motorway	l'autoroute (f)	lo-to-root
mountain	la montagne	la mo(n)-tan-ye(r)
mountaineering	l'alpinisme (m)	lal-peen-eesm
to go mountaineering	faire de l'alpinisme	fair de(r) lal-peen-eesm
mouse	la souris	la soo-ree
moustache	la moustache	la moos-tash
to have a moustache	porter la moustache	por-tay la moos-tash
mouth	la bouche	la boosh
to move in	emménager	um-ay-nazh-ay
to move out	déménager	day-may-nazh-ay
to mow the lawn	tondre la pelouse	to(n)dr la pe(r)-looz
to multiply	multiplier	mewl-tee-plee-ay
music	la musique	la mew-zeek
classical music	la musique classique	la mew-zeek klass-eek
pop music	la musique pop	la mew-zeek pop
musician (m)	le musicien	le(r) mew-zees-ee-ye(n)
musician (f)	la musicienne	la mew-zees-ee-yen
mustard	la moutarde	la moo-tard
My name is...	Je m'appelle...	zher(r) ma-pel

N

naked	nu(e)	new
name	le nom	le(r) no(m)
first name	le prénom	le(r) pray-no(m)
surname	le nom de famille	le(r) no(m) de(r) fa-mee-ye
His name is...	Il s'appelle...	eel sa-pel
My name is...	Je m'appelle...	zhe(r) ma-pel
What's your name?	Comment t'appelles-tu?	kom-a(n) ta-pel-tew

napkin	la serviette de table	la ser-vee-et de(r) tabl
narrow	étroit(e)	ay-trwa
naughty	méchant(e)	may-sha(n)
navy blue	bleu(e) marine	ble(r) mar-een
near	près de	pray de(r)
neck	le cou	le(r) koo
necklace	le collier	le(r) kol-ee-ay
needle	l'aiguille (f)	lay-gwee-ye
needlecraft shop	la mercerie	la mair-se(r)-ree
neighbour (m)	le voisin	le(r) vwa-sa(n)
neighbour (f)	la voisine	la vwa-seen
nephew	le neveu	le(r) ne(r)-ve(r)
nest	le nid	le(r) nee
net (tennis court)	le filet	le(r) fee-lay
net (fishing)	le filet	le(r) fee-lay
Netherlands	les Pays-Bas (m)	lay pay-ee-ba
new	neuf (neuve)	ne(r)f (ner(r)v)
New Year's Day	le jour de l'An	le(r) zhoor de(r) la(n)
New Year's Eve	le Réveillon	le(r) ray-vay-yo(n)
Happy New Year	Bonne année	bon a-nay
New Zealand	la Nouvelle-Zélande	la noo-vel zay-la(n)d
news	les informations (f)	layz a(n)-for-mas-yo(n)
newspaper	le journal	le(r) zhoor-nal
newspaper stand	le kiosque	le(r) key-osk
next	prochain(e)	prosh-a(n)
the next day	le lendemain	le(r) la(n)-de(r)-ma(n)
next Monday	lundi prochain	lo(n)-dee prosh-a(n)
next week	la semaine prochaine	la se(r)-mayn prosh-ayn
nice	gentil(le)	zha(n)-tee (zha(n)-tee-ye(r))
niece	la nièce	la nee-ays
night, at night	la nuit	la nwee
nightdress	la chemise de nuit	la she(r)-meez de(r) nwee
nine	neuf	ne(r)f
999 call	appeler police secours	a-pel-ay po-leess se(r)-koor
nineteen	dix-neuf	deez-ne(r)f
ninety	quatre-vingt-dix	katr-va(n)-deece
no	non	no(n)
no entry (road sign)	sens interdit	sa(n)s a(n)-ter-dee
no parking	stationnement interdit	stas-ee-on-ma(n) a(n)-ter-dee
No smoking	Non-fumeurs	no(n)-few-mer
noisy	bruyant(e)	brew-ya(n)
noodles	les nouilles (f)	lay noo-ye(r)
north	le nord	le(r) nor
North Pole	le Pôle Nord	le(r) pol nor
nose	le nez	le(r) nay
note (money)	le billet	le(r) bee-yay
nothing	rien	ree-a(n)
Nothing to declare	Rien à déclarer	ree-a(n) a day-klar-ay
novel	le roman	le(r) rom-a(n)
November	novembre	nova(m)br
now, nowadays	de nos jours	de(r) no zhoor
number plate	la plaque d'immatriculation	la plak dee-mat-rik-ew-las-ee-o(n)
nurse (m), male nurse	l'infirmier (m)	la(n)-feerm-ee-ay
nurse (f)	l'infirmière (f)	la(n)-feerm-ee-air

O

oak tree	le chêne	le(r) shayn
oar	la rame	la ram
obedient	obéissant(e)	o-bay-ees-a(n)
It is one o'clock.	Il est une heure.	eel ayt-ewn er
It is 3 o'clock.	Il est trois heures.	eel ay trwaz-er
October	octobre	ok-tobr
office	le bureau	le(r) bewr-o
offices, office block	les bureaux (m)	lay bew-ro
oil (engine/food)	l'huile (f)	lweel
old	vieux (vieille)	vee-e(r) (vee-aye)
old-fashioned	vieux-jeu	vee-e(r)-zhe(r)
old age	la vieillesse	la vee-aye-ess
older than	plus âgé(e) que	plewz azhay ke(r)
on	sur	sewr
on time	à l'heure	a ler
one	un (f: une)	a(n) (ewn)
onion	l'oignon (m)	lon-yo(n)
open	ouvert(e)	oo-vair
to open	ouvrir	oo-vreer
to open a letter	ouvrir une lettre	oo-vreer ewn letr
to open the curtains	tirer les rideaux	tee-ray lay ree-do
opera	l'opéra (f)	lop-ay-ra
operating theatre	la salle d'opération	la sal dop-ay-ra-see-o(n)
operation	l'opération (f)	lop-ay-ra-see-o(n)
opposite	en face de	a(n) fas de(r)
orange (colour)	orange	or-a(n)zh
orange (fruit)	l'orange (f)	lor-a(n)zh
orchard	le verger	le(r) vair-zhay
orchestra	l'orchestre (m)	lor-kestr
to order	commander	kom-a(n)-day
ostrich	l'autruche (f)	lo-trewsh
out (for sports)	out	out
out of	hors de	or de(r)
out of focus	flou(e)	floo
oven	le four	le(r) foor
over	par dessus	par de(r)-sew
to overtake	doubler	doo-blay
overtime	les heures (f) supplémentaires	layz er sew-play-ma(n)-tair
owl	le hibou	le(r) ee-boo

P

Pacific Ocean	le Pacifique	le(r) pa-see-feek
to pack	faire sa valise	fair sa val-eez
packet	le paquet	le(r) pa-kay
to paddle	barboter	bar-bot-ay
paint	la peinture	la pa(n)-tewr
to paint	peindre	pa(n)dr
painter	l'artiste (m/f)	lar-teest
painting	le tableau	le(r) tab-lo
pale	pâle	pale(r)
paper	le papier	le(r) pa-pee-ay
paperback	le livre de poche	le(r) leevr de(r) posh
parcel	le colis	le(r) kol-ee
parents	les parents (m)	lay par-a(n)
park	le parc	le(r) park
park keeper	le gardien	le(r) gar-dee-ya(n)

English	French	Pronunciation
to park	garer la voiture	ga-ray la vwa-tewr
no parking	stationnement interdit	stas-ee-on-e(r)-ma(n) a(n)-ter-dee
parliament	le parlement	le(r) par-le(r)-ma(n)
party (celebration)	la fête	la fayt
party (political)	le parti	le(r) par-tee
to pass an exam	être reçu(e) à un examen	et-re(r) re(r)-sew a an-ex-ama(n)
passenger (m)	le passager	le(r) pas-azh-ay
passenger (f)	la passagère	la pas-azh-air
passport	le passeport	le(r) pas-por
past	le passé	le(r) pas-ay
in the past	autrefois	otre(r)-fwa
pasta	les pâtes	lay pate(r)
pastry	la pâtisserie	la pa-tee-ser-ee
paté	le pâté	le(r) pa-tay
path (in garden or park)	l'allée (f)	lal-ay
path	le sentier	le(r) sa(n)-tee-ay
patient (m)	le blessé	le(r) bles-ay
patient (f)	la blessée	la bles-ay
pattern	le patron	le(r) pa-tro(n)
pavement	le trottoir	le(r) trot-war
paw	la patte	la pat
PE	la gymnastique	la zheem-nast-eek
pea	le petit pois	le(r) pe(r)-tee pwa
peaceful	paisible	pay-zeebl
peach	la pêche	la pesh
pear	la poire	la pwar
pedestrian (m)	le piéton	le(r) pee-ay-to(n)
pedestrian (f)	la piétonne	la pee-ayton
pedestrian crossing	le passage clouté	le(r) pas-azh kloo-tay
pen	le stylo	le(r) stee-lo
ball-point pen	le stylo-bille	le(r) stee-lo-bee-ye
pencil	le crayon	le(r) kray-yo(n)
pencil case	la trousse	la troos
penguin	le pingouin	le(r) pa(n)-goo-a(n)
pepper	le poivre	le(r) pwavr
to perch	se percher	se(r) per-shay
perfume	le parfum	le(r) par-fu(m)
petrol	l'essence (f)	lay-sa(n)s
petrol station	la station-service	la stas-ee-o(n) ser-vees
to fill up with petrol	faire le plein	fair le(r) pla(n)
petticoat, slip	le jupon	le(r) zhew-po(n)
photo, photograph	la photo	la fo-to
to take a photograph	prendre une photo	pra(n)dr ewn fo-to
photographer (m/f)	le photographe	le(r) fo-to-graf
photography	la photographie	la fo-to-graf-ee
physics	la physique	la fee-zeek
piano	le piano	le(r) pee-an-o
to play the piano	jouer du piano	zhooay dew pee-an-o
to pick	cueillir	ke(r)-yeer
to pick flowers	cueillir des fleurs	ke(r)-yeer day fler
to pick up	ramasser	ram-as-ay
to pick up the receiver	décrocher	day-krosh-ay
picnic	le pique-nique	le(r) peek-neek
pig	le cochon	le(r) kosh-o(n)
pigeon	le pigeon	le(r) pee-zho(n)
pill	le comprimé	le(r) ko(m)-pree-may
pillow	l'oreiller (m)	lor-ay-yay
pilot (m/f)	le pilote	le(r) pee-lot
pin	l'épingle (f)	lay-pa(n)gl
pink	rose	roz
pitch (for sports)	le terrain	le(r) ter-a(n)
to pitch a tent	dresser une tente	dress-ay ewn ta(n)t
planet	la planète	la plan-et
plate	l'assiette (f)	las-ee-yet
plaits	les nattes (f)	lay nat
to have plaits	avoir des nattes	a-vwar day nat
to plant	planter	pla(n)-tay
plastic	le plastique	le(r) plas-teek
made of plastic	en plastique	a(n) plas-teek
platform (station)	le quai	le(r) kay
platform ticket	le ticket de quai	le tee-kay de(r) kay
play (theatre)	la pièce de théâtre	la pee-ays de(r) tay-atr
to play , to play (an instrument)	jouer	zhoo-ay
to play cards	jouer aux cartes	zhoo-ay o kart
to play chess	jouer aux échecs	zhoo-ay oz ay-shek
to play draughts	jouer aux dames	zhoo-ay o dam
to play football	jouer au football	zhoo-ay o foot-bol
to play golf	faire du golf	fair dew golf
to play squash	jouer au squash	zhoo-ay o skwash
to play tennis	jouer au tennis	zhoo-ay o ten-ees
player (m)	le joueur	le(r) zhoor-er
player (f)	la joueuse	la zhoo-erz
playful	fou-fou	foo-foo
playground	la cour de récréation	la koor de(r) ray-kray-a-see-o(n)
Please find enclosed...	Veuillez trouver ci-joint...	ve(r)-yay troo-vay see-zhwa(n)
pleased with	content(e) de	ko(n)-ta(n) de(r)
to plough	labourer	la-boor-ay
plug (electric)	la prise	la preez
plug (bath or sink)	le bouchon	le(r) boo-sho(n)
plum	la prune	la prewn
plumber (m/f)	le plombier	le(r) plo(m)-bee-ay
plus (maths)	plus	plews
pocket	la poche	la posh
poetry	la poésie	la po-ay-zee
polar bear	l'ours (m) blanc	loors bla(n)
police	la police	la po-lees
police car	la voiture de police	la vwa-tewr de(r) po-lees
police station	le commissariat de police	le(r) kom-ee-sar-ee-a de(r) po-lees
policeman, policewoman	l'agent (m) de police	lazha(n) de(r) polees
polite	poli(e)	po-lee
politics	la politique	la pol-ee-teek
pond	le bassin	le(r) bas-a(n)
popular	populaire	pop-ew-lair
pork chop	la côte de porc	la kot de(r) por
port	le port	le(r) por
porter	le porteur	le(r) por-ter
porthole	le hublot	le(r) ew-blo
to post	mettre à la poste	metr a la post
post office	la poste	la post
postal code	le code postal	le(r) kod pos-tal
post-box	la boîte aux lettres	la bwat o letr
postcard	la carte postale	la kart pos-tal
postman/woman	le facteur	le(r) fak-ter
potato	la pomme de terre	la pom de(r) tair
to pour	verser	ver-say
powerboat	le hors-bord	le(r) or-bor
prescription	l'ordonnance (f)	lor-don-a(n)ce
present (now)	le présent	le(r) pray-za(n)
present (gift)	le cadeau	le(r) ka-do
president (m/f)	le président	le(r) pray-zee-da(n)
pretty	joli(e)	zho-lee

price	le prix	le(r) pree
prime minister (m/f)	le premier ministre	le(r) pre(r)-mee-ay mee-neestr
programme	l'émission (f)	lay-mee-see-o(n)
pudding	le dessert	le(r) day-ser
puddle	la flaque d'eau	la flak do
to take someone's pulse	prendre le pouls	pra(n)dr le(r) poo
to pull	tirer	tee-ray
pupil (m)	l'élève (m/f)	lay-lev
puppy	le petit chien	le(r) pe(r)-tee shee-a(n)
purple	violet(te)	vee-o-lay
to purr	ronronner	ro(n)-ron-ay
purse	le portemonnaie	le(r) port-mon-ay
to push	pousser	poo-say
push-chair	la poussette	la poo-set
to put	mettre	metr
to put down	déposer	day-poz-ay
to put money in the bank	mettre de l'argent en banque	metr de(r) lar-zha(n) a(n) ba(n)k
pyjamas	le pyjama	le(r) pee-zham-a

Q

a quarter	un quart	a(n) kar
a quarter past 10	dix heures et quart	deez-er ay kar
a quarter to 10	dix heures moins le quart	deez-er mwa(n) le(r) kar
question	la question	la kay-stee-o(n)
to ask a question	poser une question	po-zay ewn kay-stee-o(n)
to queue	faire la queue	fair la ke(r)
quiet, calm	calme	kalm

R

rabbit	le lapin	le(r) la-pa(n)
races, racing	les courses (f)	lay koors
racket	la raquette	la rak-et
radiator	le radiateur	le(r) ra-dee-at-er
radio	la radio	la ra-dee-o
railway	le chemin de fer	le(r) she(r)-ma(n) de(r) fair
rain	la pluie	la plew-ee
rainbow	l'arc-en-ciel (m)	lark-a(n)-see-el
raincoat	l'imperméable (m)	la(m)-per-may-abl
raindrop	la goutte de pluie	la goot de(r) plew-ee
to rain	pleuvoir	ple(r)-vwar
It's raining.	Il pleut.	eel ple(r)
rake	le rateau	le(r) ra-to
raspberry	la framboise	la fra(m)-bwaz
raw	cru(e)	krew
razor	le rasoir	le(r) raz-war
to read	lire	leer
to read a book	lire un livre	leer a(n) leevr
to read a story	lire une histoire	leer ewn eest-war
It's ready. (meal)	A table!	a tabl
receipt	le reçu	le(r) re(r)-sew
to receive	recevoir	re(r)-se-vwar
receiver	le récepteur	le(r) ray-sep-ter
reception	la réception	la ray-sep-see-o(n)

recipe	la recette	la re(r)-set
record	le disque	le(r) deesk
record player	le tourne-disque	lè(r) toorn-deesk
record shop	le marchand de disques	le(r) mar-sha(n) de(r) deesk
rectangle	le rectangle	le(r) rekt-a(n)gl
red	rouge	roozh
red (for hair colour), ginger	roux (rousse)	roo (roos)
red hair	les cheveux roux	lay she(r)-ve(r) roo
reed	le roseau	le(r) roz-o
referee	l'arbitre (m)	lar-beetr
to be related to	être parent(e) de	et-re(r) par-a(n) de(r)
to reserve	réserver	ray-ser-vay
to reserve a room	réserver une chambre	ray-zer-vay ewn sha(m)br
to reserve a seat	réserver une place	ray-zer-vay ewn plas
reserved seat	la place réservée	la plas ray-zer-vay
to rest	se reposer	se(r) re(r)-poz-ay
restaurant	le restaurant	le(r) rest-or-a(n)
to retire	prendre sa retraite	pra(n)dr sa re(r)-trayt
by return of post	par retour du courrier	par re(r)-toor dew koor-ee-ay
return ticket	le billet aller retour	le(r) bee-yay a-lay re(r)-toor
rice	le riz	le(r) ree
to ride a bicycle	aller à bicyclette	a-lay a bee-see-klet
on the right	à droite	a drwat
right side	le côté droit	le(r) ko-tay drwa
the right, right wing	la droite	la drwat
ring	la bague	la bag
to ring	sonner	son-ay
to ring the bell	sonner à la porte	son-ay a la port
ripe	mûr(e)	mewr
river	la rivière	la ree-vee-air
road	la route	la root
to roar	mugir	mew-zheer
rock	le rocher	le(r) rosh-ay
roll	le petit pain	le(r) pe(r)-tee pa(n)
roof	le toit	le(r) twa
room	la chambre	la sha(m)br
double room	la chambre pour deux personnes	la sha(m)br poor de(r) pair-son
single room	la chambre à un lit	la sha(m)br a a(n) lee
rose	la rose	la roz
roundabout (for children)	le manège	le(r) man-ayzh
to row	ramer	ram-ay
rowing boat	le canot à rames	le(r) kan-o a ram
to rub your eyes	se frotter les yeux	se(r) frot-ay layz ye(r)
rubber	la gomme	la gom
rucksack, backpack	le sac à dos	le(r) sak a do
rude	impoli(e)	a(m)-po-lee
ruler	la règle	la ray-gl
to run	courir	koo-reer
to run a bath	faire couler un bain	fair koo-lay a(n) ba(n)
to run away	s'échapper	say-shap-ay
runway	la piste	la peest
Russia	la Russie	la rew-see

S

English	French	Pronunciation
safety belt	la ceinture de sécurité	la sa(n)-tewr de(r) say-kewr-ee-tay
sailor	le marin	le(r) mar-a(n)
salad	la salade	la sal-ad
salami, French salami	le saucisson	le(r) soo-see-so(n)
salary	le salaire	le(r) sal-air
sale (in shop)	solde (m)	sold
salmon	le saumon	le(r) so-mo(n)
sales representative (m)	le représentant de commerce	le(r) re(r)-pray-za(n)-ta(n) de(r) kom-airs
sales representative (f)	la représentante de commerce	la re(r)-pray-za(n)-tant de(r) kom-airs
salt	le sel	le(r) sel
same	pareil(le)	par-aye
the same age as	le même âge que	le(r) mem azh ke(r)
sand	le sable	le(r) sabl
sandals	les sandales (f)	lay sa(n)-dal
sandcastle	le château de sable	le(r) sha-to de(r) sabl
satchel	le cartable	le(r) kart-abl
Saturday	samedi (m)	sam-dee
saucepan	la casserole	la kas-er-ol
saucer	la soucoupe	la soo-koop
sausage	la saucisse	la so-sees
saw	la scie	la see
to say	dire	deer
scales	la balance	la bal-a(n)s
Scandinavia	la Scandinavie	la ska(n)-deen-avee
scarecrow	l'épouvantail (m)	lay-poov-a(n)-tie
scarf	l'écharpe (f)	lay-sharp
scenery	le décor	le(r) day-kor
nursery school	l'école (f) maternelle	lay-kol ma-tern-el
at nursery school	à la maternelle	a la ma-tern-el
primary school	l'école (f) primaire	lay-kol pree-mair
secondary school	le collège	le kol-ezh
at (secondary) school	au collège	o kol-ezh
scissors	les ciseaux (m)	lay seez-o
to score a goal	marquer un but	mar-kay a(n) bew
screwdriver	le tournevis	le(r) toorn-vees
sea	la mer	la mair
sea food	les fruits de mer (m)	lay frwee de(r) mair
seagull	la mouette	la moo-et
to be seasick	avoir le mal de mer	a-vwar le(r) mal de(r) mair
at the seaside	au bord de la mer	o bor de(r) la mair
season	la saison	la say-zo(n)
season ticket	la carte d'abonnement	la kart dab-on-e(r)-ma(n)
seat	la place	la plas
reserved seat	la place réservée	la plas ray-zer-vay
seaweed	l'algue (f)	lalg
second (unit of time)	la seconde	la se(r)-gond
second	deuxième	de(r)-zee-aym
the second (for dates only)	le deux	le(r) de(r)
second class	deuxième classe (f)	de(r)-zee-aym klas
second floor	le deuxième étage	le(r) de(r)-zee-aym ay-tazh
secretary (m/f)	le/la secrétaire	le(r)/la se-kray-tair
See you later.	A tout à l'heure.	a toot a ler
seeds	les graines (f)	lay grayn
to sell	vendre	ve(n)dr
to send	envoyer	a(n)-voy-ay
I am sending (...) separately.	Je t'envoie (...) séparément	zhe(r) te(n) vwa say-par-ay -ma(n)
to send a postcard	envoyer une carte postale	a(n)-voy-ay ewn kart postal
to send a telegram	envoyer un télégramme	a(n)-voy-ay a(n) tay-lay-gram
sentence	la phrase	la fraz
September	septembre	sep-ta(m)br
to serve (a meal)	servir	ser-veer
to serve (in a sport)	servir	ser-veer
service	le service	le(r) ser-vees
Is service included?	Service compris?	ser-vees ko(m)-pree
Service is not included.	Service non-compris.	ser-vees no(n)-ko(m)-pree
seven	sept	set
seventeen	dix-sept	dees-set
seventy	soixante-dix	swas-a(n)t-dees
to sew	coudre	koodr
shade	l'ombre (f)	lombr
to shake	agiter	a-zhee-tay
to shake hands with	secouer la main à	se(r)-koo-ay la ma(n) a
shallow	peu profond(e)	pe(r) pro-fo(n)
shampoo	le shampooing	le(r) sham-poo-a(n)
shape	la forme	la form
to shave	se raser	se(r) ra-zay
electric shaver	le rasoir électrique	le(r) ra-zwar ay-lek-treek
shaving foam	la crème à raser	la kraym a ra-zay
sheep	le mouton	le(r) moo-to(n)
sheepdog	le chien de berger	le(r) shee-a(n) de(r) ber-zhay
sheet	le drap	le(r) dra
shell	le coquillage	le(r) ko-key-azh
to shine	briller	bree-ay
ship	le navire	le(r) na-veer
shirt	la chemise	la she(r)-meez
shoes	les chaussures (f)	lay sho-sewr
tennis shoes	les tennis (m)	lay ten-ees
shops	les magasins (m)	lay mag-az-a(n)
shop assistant (m)	le vendeur	le(r) va(n)-der
shop assistant (f)	la vendeuse	la va(n)-derz
shopkeeper (m)	le marchand	le(r) mar-sha(n)
shopkeeper (f)	la marchande	la mar-sha(n)d
shop window	la vitrine	la vee-treen
to shop at the market	faire le marché	fair le(r) mar-shay
to go shopping	faire les courses	fair lay koors
shopping bag	le sac à provisions	le(r) sak a pro-vee-zee-o(n)
short	court (e)	koor
to be short	être petit(e)	et-re(r) pe(r)-tee
shoulder	l'épaule (f)	lay-pol
to shout	crier	kree-ay
shower	la douche	la doosh
to have a shower	prendre une douche	pra(n)dr ewn doosh
shut	fermé(e)	fer-may
shy	timide	tee-meed
to be sick	vomir	vom-eer
side	le côté	le(r) ko-tay
to sightsee	visiter	vee-zee-tay
signpost	le poteau indicateur	le(r) po-to a(n)-dee-kat-er
silly	idiot(e)	ee-dee-o

English	French	Pronunciation
silver	l'argent (m)	lar-zha(n)
made of silver	en argent	a(n) ar-zha(n)
to sing	chanter	sha(n)-tay
to sing out of tune	chanter faux	sha(n)-tay fo
singer (m)	le chanteur	le(r) sha(n)-ter
singer (f)	la chanteuse	la sha(n)-terz
a single room	une chambre à un lit	ewn sha(m)br a a(n) lee
sink	l'évier (m)	lay-vee-ay
sister	la soeur	la ser
to sit an exam	passer un examen	pa-say a(n) e-xam-a(n)
to sit by the fire	s'asseoir au coin du feu	sa-swar o kwa(n) dew fe(r)
to sit down	s'asseoir	sa-swar
to be sitting down	être assis(e)	et-re(r) a-see
six	six	sees
sixteen	seize	sayz
sixty	soixante	swas-a(n)t
size	la taille	la ta-ye
What size is this?	C'est quelle taille?	say kel ta-ye
skis	les skis (m)	lay skee
ski boots	les chaussures (f) de ski	lay sho-sewr de(r) skee
ski instructor (m)	le moniteur	le(r) mon-ee-ter
ski instructor (f)	la monitrice	la mon-ee-trees
ski pole	le bâton de ski	le(r) ba-to(n) de(r) skee
ski resort	la station de ski	la sta-see-o(n) de(r) skee
ski slope, ski run	la piste	la peest
to go skiing	faire du ski	fair dew skee
skilful, good with your hands	adroit(e)	a-drwa
skin	la peau	la po
skirt	la jupe	la zhewp
sky	le ciel	le(r) see-el
skyscraper	le gratte-ciel	le(r) grat-see-el
sledge	la luge	la lewzh
to sleep	dormir	dor-meer
Sleep well.	Dormez-bien.	dor-may bee-a(n)
sleeping-car	le wagon-lit	le(r) wago(n)-lee
sleeping bag	le sac de couchage	le(r) sak de(r) koosh-azh
to be sleepy	avoir sommeil	avwar som-aye
slide	le toboggan	le(r) to-bog-a(n)
slim	mince	ma(n)ce
to slip	glisser	glee-say
slippers	les pantoufles (f)	lay pa(n)-toofl
slope	la pente	la pa(n)t
slow	lent(e)	la(n)
to slow down	ralentir	ra-la(n)-teer
small	petit(e)	pe(r)-tee
small (clothes size)	petit	pe(r)tee
to smile	sourire	soo-reer
smoke	la fumée	la few-may
snake	le serpent	le(r) sair-pa(n)
to sneeze	éternuer	ay-ter-new-ay
to snore	ronfler	ro(n)-flay
snow	la neige	la nezh
It's snowing.	Il neige.	eel nezh
snowman	le bonhomme de neige	le(r) bon-om de(r) nezh
soaked to the skin	trempé(e) jusqu'aux os	tra(m)-pay zhews-koz-o
soap	le savon	le(r) sa-vo(n)
society	la société	la so-see-ay-tay
socks	les chaussettes (f)	lay sho-set
sofa	le canapé	le(r) kan-a-pay
soft	doux (douce)	doo (doos)
soil	la terre	la tair
soldier	le soldat	le(r) sol-da
sole	la sole	la sol
someone	quelqu'un	kel-ka(n)
son	le fils	le(r) fees
only son	le fils unique	le(r) fees ew-neek
to sort, to sort out, to arrange	trier	tree-ay
soup	le potage	le(r) pot-azh
south	le sud	le(r) sewd
South America	l'Amérique (f) du Sud	lam-air-eek dew sewd
South Pole	le Pôle Sud	le(r) pol sewd
to sow	semer	se(r)-may
space	l'espace (m)	less-pass
spaceship	l'engin (m) spacial	la(n)-zha(n) spas-ee-al
spade	la bêche	la besh
spade (smaller spade or toy)	la pelle	la pel
Spain	l'Espagne (f)	less-pan-ye
Spanish (language or subject)	l'espagnol (m)	less-pan-yol
sparrow	le moineau	le(r) mwa-no
spelling	l'orthographe (f)	lor-to-graf
to spend money	dépenser de l'argent	day-pa(n)-say de(r) lar-zha(n)
spices	les épices (f)	layz ay-peece
spider	l'araignée (f)	la-rayn-yay
spinach	les épinards (m)	layz-ay-peen-ar
to splash	éclabousser	ay-kla-boo-say
spoon	la cuillère	la kwee-yair
sport	le sport	le(r) spor
sports equipment	l'équipement (m) de sport	lay-keep-ma(n) de(r) spor
spotlight	le projecteur	le(r) prozh-ek-ter
spotted	à pois	a pwa
to sprain your wrist	se fouler le poignet	se(r) foo-lay le(r) pwan-yay
spring	le printemps	le(r) pra(n)-ta(n)
square (shape)	le carré	le(r) kar-ay
square (in a town)	la place	la plas
to play squash	jouer au squash	zhoo-ay o skwash
squirrel	l'écureuil (m)	lay-kew-roye
stable	l'écurie (f)	lay-kewr-ee
stage (theatre)	la scène	la sayn
staircase, stairs	l'escalier (m)	lay-skal-ee-ay
stamp	le timbre	le(r) ta(m)br
to stand up	se lever	se(r) le(r)-vay
to be standing	être debout	et-re(r) de(r)-boo
star	l'étoile (f)	lay-twal
to start off (in vehicle)	démarrer	day-mar-ay
starter (meal)	l'entrée (f)	la(n)-tray
station	la gare	la gar
statue	la statue	la stat-ew
to stay in a hotel	rester à l'hôtel	ray-stay a lo-tel
steak	le biftek	le(r) beef-tek
to steal	voler	vo-lay
steep	escarpé(e)	ay-skar-pay
steering wheel	le volant	le(r) vol-a(n)
to stick	coller	ko-lay
sticking plaster	le sparadrap	le(r) spa-ra-dra
to sting	piquer	pee-kay
stomach	l'estomac (m)	less-tom-a
to have stomach ache	avoir mal au ventre	a-vwar mal o va(n)tr
story	l'histoire (f)	lees-twar

stove	le réchaud	*le(r) ray-sho*				
straight (for hair)	raide	*rayd*				
straight hair	les cheveux raides	*lay she(r)-ve(r) rayd*		**T**		
to go straight on	aller tout droit	*a-lay too drwa*				
strawberry	la fraise	*la frayz*	table	la table	*la tabl*
stream	le ruisseau	*le(r) rwee-so*	bedside table	la table de chevet	*la tabl de(r) she(r)-vay*
street	la rue	*la rew*			
street light	le réverbère	*le(r) ray-vairb-air*	to lay the table	mettre le couvert	*maitre(r) le(r) koo-vair*
side street	la rue	*la rew*			
one way street	le sens unique	*le(r) sa(n)s ew-neek*	tablecloth	la nappe	*la nap*
to stretch	s'étirer	*say-tee-ray*	tail	la queue	*la ke(r)*
stretcher	le brancard	*le(r) bra(n)-kar*	to take	prendre	*pra(n)dr*
striped	à rayures	*a ray-yewr*	to take the bus	prendre l'autobus	*pra(n)dr lo-to-bews*
strong	fort(e)	*for*	to take a	prendre une photo	*pra(n)dr ewn fo-to*
student (m)	l'étudiant (m)	*lay-tew-dee-a(n)*	photograph		
student (f)	l'étudiante (f)	*lay-tew-dee-a(n)t*	to take someone's	prendre le pouls	*pra(n)dr le(r) poo*
to study	étudier	*ay-tew-dee-ay*	pulse		
subject (of study)	la matière	*la ma-tee-air*	to take someone's	prendre la	*pra(n)dr la ta(m)-*
to subtract	soustraire	*soo-strair*	temperature	température	*pay-ra-tewr*
suburb	la banlieue	*la ba(n)-lee-ye(r)*	to take off	décoller	*day-kol-ay*
subway	le passage	*le(r) pass-azh soo-*	to take out ,to	retirer	*re(r)-teer-ay*
	souterrain	*ter-a(n)*	draw		
sugar	le sucre	*le(r) sewkr*	to take money out	retirer de l'argent	*re(r)-teer-ay de(r) lar-zha(n)*
suitcase	la valise	*la val-eez*			
summer	l'été (f)	*lay-tay*	to be tall	être grand(e)	*et-re(r) gra(n)*
summit	le sommet	*le(r) som-ay*	tame	apprivoisé(e)	*a-pree-vwa-zay*
sun	le soleil	*le(r) sol-aye*	tanned	bronzé(e)	*bro(n)-zay*
The sun is shining.	Le soleil brille.	*le(r) sol-aye bree-ye*	tap	le robinet	*le(r) rob-ee-nay*
			to tap your feet	taper du pied	*ta-pay dew pee-ay*
to sunbathe	se bronzer	*se(r) bro(n)-zay*	tart	la tarte	*la tart*
Sunday	dimanche (m)	*dee-ma(n)sh*	taste, flavour	le goût	*le(r) goo*
sunglasses	les lunettes (f) de	*lay lewn-et de(r)*	to taste, to try	goûter	*goo-tay*
	soleil	*sol-aye*	It tastes good.	C'est très bon.	*say tray bo(n)*
sunrise	le lever du soleil	*le(r) le(r)-vay dew sol-aye*	taxes	les impôts (m)	*layz a(m)po*
			taxi	le taxi	*le(r) taksee*
sunset	le coucher du soleil	*le(r) koo-shay dew sol-aye*	to hail a taxi	appeler un taxi	*a-pel-ay a(n) taksee*
			taxi-driver (m/f)	le chauffeur de taxi	*le(r) sho-fer de(r) taksee*
sunshade	le parasol	*le(r) pa-ra-sol*			
suntan lotion	la crème solaire	*la kraym sol-air*	taxi rank	la station de taxis	*la sta-see-o(n) de(r) taksee*
supermarket	le supermarché	*le(r) sew-pair-mar-shay*			
to go to the	aller au	*a-lay o sew-pair-*	tea	le thé	*le(r) tay*
supermarket	supermarché	*mar-shay*	tea towel	le torchon	*le(r) tor-sho(n)*
supper	le dîner	*le(r) dee-nay*	to teach	enseigner	*a(n)-sayn-yay*
surgeon (m/f)	le chirurgien	*le(r) sheer-ewr-zhee-a(n)*	teacher (m/f)	le professeur	*le(r) prof-ay-sir*
			team	l'équipe (f)	*lay-keep*
surname	le nom de famille	*le(r) no(m) de(r) fa-mee-ye*	teapot	la théière	*la tay-yair*
			to tear	déchirer	*day-sheer-ay*
to sweat	transpirer	*tra(n)s-peeray*	telegram	le télégramme	*le(r) tay-lay-gram*
sweet, charming	mignon(ne)	*meen-yo(n)*	telephone	le téléphone	*le(r) tay-lay-fon*
sweet (sugary)	sucré(e)	*sew-kray*	telephone area	l'indicatif (m)	*la(n)-dee-kat-eef*
sweet-smelling	parfumé(e)	*par-fewm-ay*	code		
to swim	nager	*na-zhay*	telephone box	la cabine	*la ka-been tay-lay-*
to swim, to have a	se baigner	*se(r) bayn-yay*		téléphonique	*fon-eek*
swim			telephone	l'annuaire (m)	*la-new-air*
swimming pool	la piscine	*la pee-seen*	directory		
swing	la balançoire	*la ba-la(n)-swar*	telephone number	le numéro de	*le(r) new-mair-o*
to switch the light	éteindre	*ay-ta(n)dr*		téléphone	*de(r) tay-lay-fon*
off			to answer the	répondre au	*ray-po(n)-dro tay-*
to switch the light	allumer	*a-lewm-ay*	telephone	téléphone	*lay-fon*
on			to make a phone	composer le numéro	*kom-po-zay le(r)*
Switzerland	la Suisse	*la swees*	call, to dial		*new-mair-o*
			telescope	le télescope	*le(r) tay-lay-skop*
			television	la télévision	*la tay-lay-vee-zee-o(n)*
			to have a	avoir de la fièvre	*a-vwar de(r) la fee-yaivr*
			temperature		
			to take someone's	prendre la	*pra(n)dr la ta(m)-*
			temperature	température	*pay-ra-tewr*
			ten	dix	*dees*

125

English	French	Pronunciation
tenant (m/f)	le/la locataire	le(r)/la lok-a-tair
tennis	le tennis	le(r) tay-nees
tennis court	le court de tennis	le(r) koor de(r) tay-nees
tennis shoes	les tennis (m)	lay tay-nees
to play tennis	jouer au tennis	zhoo-ay o tay-nees
tent	la tente	la ta(n)t
term	le trimestre	le(r) tree-mestr
to thank	remercier	re-mair-see-yay
Thank you for your letter of...	Je vous remercie de votre lettre du...	zhe(r) voo re(r)-mair-see de(r) votr letr dew
Thank you very much.	Merci beaucoup.	mair-see bo-koo
That will be.../cost...	Ça fait...	sa fay
to thaw	fondre	fo(n)dr
theatre	le théâtre	le(r) tay-atre(r)
thermometer	le thermomètre	le(r) tair-mo-maytre(r)
thin	maigre	may-gre(r)
Thinking of you.	Je pense bien à toi.	zhe(r) pa(n)s bee-an-a twa
third	troisième	trwa-zee-em
a third	un tiers	a(n) tee-air
the third (for dates only)	le trois	le(r) trwa
thirteen	treize	trayz
thirty	trente	tra(n)t
to be thirsty	avoir soif	avwar swaf
this evening	ce soir	se(r) swar
this morning	ce matin	se(r) ma-ta(n)
a thousand	mille	meel
thread	le fil	le(r) feel
three	trois	trwa
three quarters	les trois quarts	lay trwa kar
through	à travers	a tra-ver
to throw	lancer	la(n)-say
thrush	la grive	la greev
thumb	le pouce	le(r) poos
thunder	le tonnerre	le(r) ton-air
thunder storm	l'orage (m)	lor-azh
Thursday	jeudi (m)	zhe(r)-dee
ticket	le billet	le(r) bee-yay
airline ticket	le billet d'avion	le(r) bee-yay da-vee-o(n)
platform ticket	le ticket de quai	le(r) tee-kay de(r) kay
return ticket	le billet aller retour	le(r) bee-yay a-lay re(r)-toor
season ticket	la carte d'abonnement	la kart da-bon-e(r)-ma(n)
ticket collector (m)	le contrôleur	le(r) ko(n)-trol-er
ticket collector (f)	la contrôleuse	la ko(n)-trol-erz
ticket machine	le distributeur automatique	le(r) dee-streeb-ew-ter oto-ma-teek
ticket office	le guichet	le(r) gee-shay
to tidy up	ranger ses affaires	ra(n)-zhay sayza-fair
tie	la cravate	la krav-at
tiger	le tigre	le(r) tee-gr
tight	serré(e)	say-ray
tights	les collants (m)	lay col-a(n)
time	le temps	le(r) ta(n)
on time	à l'heure	a ler
to be on time	arriver à l'heure	a-ree-vay a ler
What time is it?	Quelle heure est-il?	kel er ay-teel
times (maths)	fois	fwa
timetable (for transport)	l'horaire (f)	lor-air
timetable (studies or work)	l'emploi du temps	la(m)-plwa dew ta(m)
tin	la boîte	la bwat
tinned food	les conserves (f)	lay ko(n)-serv
tiny	minuscule	mee-new-skewl
tip	le pourboire	le(r) poor-bwar
to, towards	vers	vair
today	aujourd'hui	o-zhoor-dwee
toe	le doigt de pied	le(r) dwa de(r) pee-ay
together	ensemble	a(n)-sa(m)bl
toilet	les toilettes (f)	lay twa-let
tomato	la tomate	la tom-at
tomorrow	demain	de(r)-ma(n)
tomorrow evening	demain soir	de(r)-ma(n) swar
tomorrow morning	demain matin	de(r)-ma(n) ma-ta(n)
tongue	la langue	la la(n)g
tooth	la dent	la da(n)
to have toothache	avoir mal aux dents	avwar mal o da(n)
toothbrush	la brosse à dents	la bros a da(n)
toothpaste	le dentifrice	le(r) da(n)-tee-frees
tortoise	la tortue	la tor-tew
to touch	toucher	too-shay
tourist (m/f)	le/la touriste	le(r)/la too-reest
towel	la serviette	la ser-vee-et
town	la ville	la veel
town centre	le centre-ville	le(r) sa(n)-tre(r) veel
town hall	l'hôtel (m) de ville	lo-tel de(r) veel
toy	le jouet	le(r) zhoo-ay
track	la voie	la vwa
tracksuit	le survêtement	le(r) sewr-vet-ma(n)
tractor	le tracteur	le(r) trak-ter
trade union	le syndicat	le(r) sa(n)-dee-ka
traffic	la circulation	la seer-kewl-a-see-o(n)
traffic jam	l'embouteillage (m)	la(m)-boo-taye-azh
traffic lights	les feux (m)	lay fe(r)
train	le train	le(r) tra(n)
The train from...	Le train en provenance de...	le(r) tra(n) a(n) pro-ve(r)-na(n)s de(r)
The train to...	Le train à destination de...	le(r) tra(n) a des-tee-na-see-o(n) de(r)
inter-city train	le rapide	le(r) ra-peed
goods train	le train de marchandises	le(r) tra(n) de(r) mar-sha(n)-deez
to travel by boat, to sail	aller en bateau	a-lay o(n) ba-to
traveller (m)	le voyageur	le(r) vwa-yazh-er
traveller (f)	la voyageuse	la vwa-yazh-erz
tray	le plateau	le(r) pla-to
tree	l'arbre (m)	larbr
triangle	le triangle	le(r) tree-a(n)gl
trolley	le chariot	le(r) shar-ee-o
trousers	le pantalon	le(r) pa(n)-tal-o(n)
trout	la truite	la trweet
trowel	la truelle	la trew-el
true	vrai(e)	vray
trumpet	la trompette	la trom-pet
to play the trumpet	jouer de la trompette	zhoo-ay de(r) la trom-pet
trunk (elephant's)	la trompe	la tromp
T-shirt	le tee-shirt	le(r) tee-shirt
Tuesday	mardi (m)	mar-dee
Tuesday the second of June	le mardi deux juin	le(r) mar-dee de(r) zhwa(n)
tulip	la tulipe	la tew-leep
tune	l'air (m)	lair
to turn	tourner	toorn-ay

to turn left	tourner à gauche	toorn-ay a gosh
to turn right	tourner à droite	toorn-ay a drwat
tusk	la défense	la day-fa(n)s
twelve	douze	dooz
twenty	vingt	va(n)
twin brother	le jumeau	le(r) zhew-mo
twin sister	la jumelle	la zhew-mel
twins, twin brothers	les jumeaux (m)	lay zhew-mo
two	deux	de(r)
tyre	le pneu	le(r) pne(r)
to have a flat tyre	avoir un pneu crevé	avwar a(n) pne(r) cre(r)-vay

U

umbrella	le parapluie	le(r) para-plwee
uncle	l'oncle (m)	lo(n)kl
under	sous	soo
underground	le métro	le(r) may-tro
underground station	la station de métro	la sta-see-o(n) de(r) may-tro
underpants (men's)	le caleçon	le(r) kal-so(n)
underpants (boys')	la culotte	la kew-lot
to get undressed	se déshabiller	se(r) day-za-bee-yay
unemployment	le chômage	le(r) sho-mazh
United States	les Etats-Unis (m)	layz ay-ta zew-nee
universe	l'univers (m)	lewn-ee-vair
to unload	décharger	day-shar-zhay
up	en haut	a(n) o
to get up	se lever	se(r) le(r)-vay
upstairs	en haut	a(n) o
to go upstairs	monter l'escalier	mo(n)-tay less-ka-lee-ay
Urgent message stop phone home stop	Message urgent stop appelle maison	may-sazh ewr-zha(n) stop a-pel may-zo(n)
useful	utile	ew-teel
usherette	l'ouvreuse (f)	loovr-erz

V

to vacuum	passer l'aspirateur	pa-say la-speer-a-ter
valley	la vallée	la va-lay
van	la camionnette	la cam-ee-o-net
veal	le veau	le(r) vo
vegetable patch	le jardin potager	le zhar-da(n) po-tazh-ay
vegetables	les légumes (m)	lay lay-gewm
Very well, thank you. (Answer to "How are you?")	Très bien, merci.	tray bee-a(n) mair-see
vest	la chemise de corps	la she(r)-meez de(r) kor
vicar	le curé	le(r) kew-ray
video	le magnétoscope	le(r) man-yet-o-skop
video camera	la caméra	la kam-ay-ra
view	la vue	la vew
village	le village	le(r) vee-lazh
vine	la vigne	la veen-ye
vinegar	le vinaigre	le(r) vee-nay-gr

vineyard	le vignoble	le(r) veen-yobl
violin	le violon	le(r) vee-o-lo(n)
to play the violin	jouer du violon	zhoo-ay dew vee-o-lo(n)
volume	le volume	le(r) vol-ewm
to vote	voter	vo-tay

W

to wag its tail	remuer la queue	re(r)-mew-ay la ke(r)
to wait for	attendre	a-ta(n)dr
waiter (m)	le garçon	le(r) gar-so(n)
waiting-room	la salle d'attente	la sal da-ta(n)t
waitress	la serveuse	la ser-verz
to wake up	se réveiller	se(r) ray-vay-yay
walk	la promenade	la pro-me(r)-nad
to go for a walk	faire une promenade	fair ewn pro-me(r)-nad
to walk	marcher	mar-shay
to walk, to go on foot	aller à pied	a-lay a pee-ay
to walk barefoot	marcher pieds nus	mar-shay pee-ay new
to take the dog for a walk	promener le chien	pro-me(r)-nay le(r) shee-a(n)
wall	le mur	le(r) mewr
wallet	le portefeuille	le(r) port-fe(r)-ye
to wash, to have a wash	faire sa toilette	fair sa twa-let
to wash up	faire la vaisselle	fair la vay-sel
to wash your hair	se laver les cheveux	se(r) la-vay lay she(r)-ve(r)
the washing	la lessive	la lay-seev
washing line	la corde à linge	la kord a la(n)zh
washing machine	la machine à laver	la ma-sheen a la-vay
to do the washing	faire la lessive	fair la lay-seev
wasp	la guêpe	la gayp
to watch television	regarder la télévision	re(r)-gar-day la tay-lay-vee-zee-o(n)
watch	la montre	la mo(n)tr
water	l'eau (f)	lo
mineral water	l'eau (f) minérale	lo mee-nay-ral
watering can	l'arrosoir (m)	la-roz-war
to waterski	faire du ski nautique	fair dew skee no-tik
wave	la vague	la vag
way, path	le chemin	le(r) she(r)-ma(n)
to ask the way	demander le chemin	de(r)-ma(n)-day le(r) she(r)-ma(n)
Which way is…?	Pour aller à…?	poor a-lay a
weak	faible	faybl
to wear	porter	por-tay
to wear glasses	porter des lunettes	por-tay day lew-net
weather	le temps	le(r) ta(m)
weather forecast	la météo	la may-tay-o
What is the weather like?	Quel temps fait-il?	kel ta(n) fay-teel
wedding	les noces (f)	lay nos
wedding ring	l'alliance (f)	la-lee-a(n)s
Wednesday	mercredi (m)	mair-kre(r)-dee
weed	la mauvaise herbe	la mo-vayz airb
to weed	désherber	dayz-airb-ay
week	la semaine	la se(r)-mayn
week-end	le week-end	le(r) week-end
weeping willow	le saule pleureur	le(r) sole pler-er

to weigh	peser	pe(r)-zay
to weigh yourself	se peser	se(r) pe(r)-zay
weight	le poids	le(r) pwa
well	bien	bee-a(n)
to have eaten well	avoir bien mangé	avwar bee-a(n) ma(n)-zhay
Very well, thank you. (answer to "How are you?")	Très bien, merci.	tray bee-a(n) mair-see
wellington boots	les bottes (f) de caoutchouc	lay bot de(r) cow-tshoo
west	l'ouest (m)	loo-est
What is the weather like?	Quel temps fait-il?	kel ta(m) fay-teel
What size is this?	C'est quelle taille?	say kel tie-ye
What time is it?	Quelle heure est-il?	kel er ay-teel
What's your name?	Comment t'appelles-tu?	koma(n) ta-pel tew
What would you like?	Que désirez-vous?	ke(r) day-zee-ray voo
wheat	le blé	le(r) blay
wheel	la roue	la roo
wheelbarrow	la brouette	la broo-et
Which way is...?	Pour aller à...?	poor a-lay a
to whisper	chuchoter	shew-shot-ay
white	blanc (blanche)	bla(n) (bla(n)sh)
Who's speaking? (on telephone)	Qui est à l'appareil?	kee ay ta la-par-aye
width	la largeur	la lar-zher
wife	la femme	la fam
wild	sauvage	so-vazh
wild flowers	les fleurs (f) sauvages	lay fler so-vazh
to win	gagner	gan-yay
wind	le vent	le(r) va(n)
window	la fenêtre	la fe-netr
to go window-shopping	faire du lèche-vitrines	fair dew lesh vee-treen
window display, shop window	la vitrine	la vee-treen
windscreen	le pare-brise	le(r) par-breez
to windsurf	faire de la planche à voile	fair de(r) la pla(n)sh a vwal
It's windy.	Il fait du vent.	eel fay dew va(n)
wine	le vin	le va(n)
wing	l'aile (f)	lay-l
winter	l'hiver (m)	lee-vair
to wipe	essuyer	ay-swee-yay
with	avec	a-vek
with balcony	avec balcon	a-vek bal-ko(n)
with bathroom	avec salle de bain	a-vek sal de(r) ba(n)
without	sans	sa(n)
woman	la femme	la fam
wood	le bois	le(r) bwa

wooden, made of wood	en bois	a(n) bwa
woodwork	la menuiserie	la men-wee-ze(r)-ee
wool	la laine	la lane
woollen	en laine	a(n) lane
word	le mot	le(r) mo
to work	travailler	tra-vie-yay
to go to work	aller travailler	a-lay tra-vie-yay
worker (m)	l'ouvrier (m)	loo-vree-yay
worker (f)	l'ouvrière (f)	loo-vree-yair
world	le monde	le(r) mond
I would like...	Je voudrais...	zhe(r) voo-dray
wrapping	l'emballage (m)	la(m)-bal-azh
to write	écrire	ay-kreer
to write a cheque	faire un chèque	fair a(n) shek
to write a letter	écrire une lettre	ay-kreer ewn letr
wrist	le poignet	le(r) pwan-yay
writing paper	le papier à lettres	le(r) pa-pee-ay a letr

Y

to yawn	bâiller	ba-yay
year	l'année (f)	la-nay
yellow	jaune	zhon
yes	oui	wee
yesterday	hier	ee-yer
yesterday evening	hier soir	ee-yer swar
yesterday morning	hier matin	ee-yer ma-ta(n)
yoghurt	le yaourt	le(r) ya-oort
young	jeune	zhe(r)n
younger than	plus jeune que	plew zhe(r)n ke(r)
Yours faithfully,	Je vous prie de croire, Monsieur/Madame, à mes sentiments les meilleurs.	zhe(r) voo pree de(r) krwar me(r)s-ye(r)/madam a may sa(n)tee-ma(n) lay may-yer

Z

zebra	le zèbre	le(r) zay-br
zero	zéro	zay-ro
zip	la fermeture éclair	la fer-me(r)-tewr ay-klair
zoo	le zoo	le(r) zo
zoo keeper (m)	le gardien de zoo	le(r) gar-dee-a(n) de(r) zo
zoo keeper (f)	la gardienne de zoo	la gar-dee-en de(r) zo

First published in 1988 by Usborne Publishing Ltd
Usborne House, 83-85 Saffron Hill
London EC1N 8RT, England.
Copyright © 1988 Usborne Publishing Ltd.

The name Usborne and the device 🎈 are Trade Marks of Usborne Publishing Ltd.